The Emotionally Available Partner

A Journey to True Love

Marian Lindner

To my husband Charles.
Thank you for being my emotionally available partner.
Your support of this project means so much to me.
I love you for all that you are.

Acknowledgements

I owe a debt of gratitude to HP for helping me to face myself, to heal, and for writing this book with me. I also want to deeply thank Carol Emery Normandi and Lauralee Roark for their amazing work on eating disorders that changed my life, and for their support of this project. *Beyond Hunger: End Your Obsession with Food and Weight* inspired this book and many of the original ideas are from Carol and Lauralee. Thank you to my wonderful husband Charles. I am so happy this work led me to you. You are more amazing than I could have ever imagined. A big thank you also goes out to Hillary Flye for her amazing, generous, and profound work with me. And also, to all the wonderful women who informed this book: Diane Conway with her wonderful book *The Fairy Godmother's Guide to Dating and Mating*, Marilyn Geist, Tami, Meg Lopez-Cepero, Lydia Yinger, Rosemary, and Anne. Thank you all so much! And for all the men who helped on my journey: Dave, Ray, Eric, Jerry, Jim, John, Mike M., thank you for all your kindness. Thanks also to my dear parents, Eleanor and Roland. The support of all my friends and family on this journey, and all the wonderful people I interacted with to get the practice I needed to do the research for this book, has worked a miracle in me. I am grateful to you all.

CONTENTS

Phase I

♥♥♥♥

Understanding

Ourselves

Preface

Connecting in intimate partnerships without shutting down emotionally has always challenged me. In 2001 when a difficult relationship ended painfully, I clearly saw how my pattern of choosing unavailable partners had left me stuck in self-hatred. Unable to let in a loving person, I realized that I needed to change. I could no longer simply point the finger and label my "ex" the problem. Profoundly sad at my inability to maintain a healthy relationship, to marry, and to start a family, I had to face the fact that I was contributing to the challenges in my relationships. And I know that I am in good company. Many women today can't commit and achieve cultural "success," feel demoralized, and live lives that revolve around other people: controlling them, avoiding them, fearing them, or blaming them.

At that time, I decided once and for all to work through my own fears of partnership. To heal, I set out to vigorously re-conceptualize my ideas about relationships. It has been quite a journey. I began by trusting all of my behaviors and observing myself non-judgmentally. I got help from a professional therapist who has been happily married for over twenty years. I talked to women who were involved in partnerships I admired. Because I had previously recovered from a very serious eating disorder, I also applied anti-diet principles to the relationship issues I was facing. I substituted obsessions with people, partnerships, and sex for the compulsive eating behaviors those self-help books addressed.

I now believe that whenever we form relationships with unavailable people, or become relationship anorexics in order to push away available people, our own partnership issues have popped up. I learned that our relationship fears are not manifesting to destroy any hope we have of maintaining a good relationship, though. These issues are only attempting to return us to the natural partner inside that already knows how to love. We are not involved in unfulfilling relationships because we are flawed; we only need to remember our essential nature. We can't be anything else but a loving partner. That is why our challenges with intimacy have been so painful for us. Each challenge we experience is actually a call from our deepest power. It urgently sends the same message from inside over and over: that each of us is loveable and good enough for a wonderful relationship right now.

I learned that the solution to my problem is inside of me, not in someone else. With this book, I have not written a rulebook on how to capture a partner or keep them, provided guidelines on controlling our behavior around potential partners, or supplied a prescription for marriage. This book functions as a guidebook for reclaiming the natural partner inside of us. Although I lead workshops on emotional

1

availability throughout California, I am not a licensed therapist. These are my personal ideas, what have worked for me, and what I continue to strive to embody. Please use your own guidance as you read this book. This is only one path to healing and it does not have to be the path for every woman. This book is based on my own experience, so please take what you like and leave the rest. I also want to point out that since I wrote the book from my perspective, it is geared toward women; however, men can also benefit from the messages. I have found that these principles transcend all barriers—including gender.

From doing this work and incorporating the wisdom of the many brave women who have walked before me, I know that it is possible to live without fleeing from intimacy. Now, after a few years of practicing the ideas in this book I am in touch with the natural partner inside of me, am happily married to a wonderful, available man, interact with him lovingly, look behind the obsession to see what is truly going on when I get emotionally shaky, and no longer need to use people for a romantic "fix" when I am upset or uncomfortable. My hope is to plant a seed that there is a solution for women, and that sharing what I have learned will help you heal faster. Any woman who struggles with fears of intimacy and partnership will discover daily support and companionship in *The Emotionally Available Partner: A Journey to True Love*.

This book contains 365 inspirational messages that are organized day by day into phases and chapters. The book may be started at the beginning; however, some women will find more benefit by searching out specific topics. Feel free to begin wherever you like. Whatever way this guidebook is utilized, the process works. By healing, our work will move out from our romantic partnerships to all of our relationships, and will help in the movement to empower women. Please join me today to celebrate ourselves and others as we let in the love of an emotionally available partner.

-Marian Lindner

·1·

Why We Choose the
Unavailable Type

In this chapter, you will uncover the reasons that you have chosen unavailable partners. You will learn about patterns established in your early childhood, behaviors that you developed to deal with your feelings, how cultural pressures influence you, and that your relationship issues are not your enemy. Enjoy the process of self-discovery. You are on your way to true love!

Day 1

Ego

I let go of my ego. Ego is equal to "edging God out." It is the extreme force of will. Most of us are terrified of letting go of our egos. We feel that without hoarding things and people, we will be swept away and end up with nothing. Basically our egos create categories because it feels safer to be special, the smartest, the best, the prettiest. If we know where we fit in these categories, we think we can predict outcomes. We think we are safe. But when we view the world through the eyes of our ego, there is no love or spontaneity. There is no Higher Power. A category is not reality. Now as we heal, we see that to be connected to the whole, to the universe, to a Higher Power, and to each other, is true safety. We are all interconnected, women and men. We are not just subjects looking at other people as objects. A partner is not a trophy. Now we know that putting ourselves in a box and defining others with reference to ourselves is a signal **we** are off balance. Conceiving of ourselves as separate puts pressure on us. Today let's make a choice to heal our partnership issues and release our egos. **I let go of my ego; I let real love in.**

Day 2

Basic Rights

Letting myself be with whoever I want, as I want, is a basic right. Who took our basic love rights away? Often we can vividly remember times we were told not to feel as we did, told how to act like a lady, and told how to manipulate others to get what we wanted. We were told these untruths sometimes by very well-meaning people who believed they were teaching us essential skills for relating. Healing, however, means that we give ourselves the permission to be with whom we want, as we want, when we want to be with them. Obviously we need a person's permission, yet to the extent that it is possible healing our partnership issues means that we take back our rights. Every human being deserves to be authentic in making love choices. This process reinstates our rights. Today, we release societal and parental influences; we know our rights. **I have the basic right to let myself love.**

Day 3

Self-Hatred

I abstain from all self-hatred today. Self-hatred can stop us in our tracks. Self-hatred tells us we are wrong, bad, hopeless, and not enough. The self-hatred cycle is powerful and ancient within many of us; however, if we examine the self-hatred cycle clearly, we see that it is actually a great distraction from our feelings. Whenever we get upset at ourselves and start to flagellate ourselves, we feel that we are doing something constructive. We feel we aren't powerless over the situation. We feel that we will just shape-up in the future so this will never be an issue again. Then we are so focused on how bad we feel after we've beaten ourselves into a pulp that whatever feeling or situation started the self-hatred ball rolling will be on the back burner. Today we recognize self-hatred for what it really is—a great distraction from what is going on within us. Then we let go of self-hatred. **When I notice myself in self-hatred, I look behind it to see the feelings surfacing in me.**

Day 4

Obsession

I look behind obsession. The detour into obsessing on another person has been a wonderful catch-all for many of us throughout our lives. When we hit adolescence, our lives usually became more complicated on many levels. We were developing womanly body characteristics and receiving more attention from people. Our parents may also have had complex relationships to our growth. School, family, and peer issues may have surfaced at this time, too. Many of us learned early that focusing on other people and dreams of partnership would distract us from feelings we didn't know how to handle in any other way. Of course, we were probably just very curious about potential partners; however, when obsession began to dominate our lives we lost our balance. Now whenever we are consistently thinking about a particular person or worried about marriage or partnership, we can be reasonably sure that we are experiencing a feeling we don't know how to cope with. Obsession is a great signal that something is going on within us. It signals that we are experiencing an emotion we don't know how to process. Today we heal by delving into our feelings to see what our preoccupations are telling us. **Today I look at my feelings whenever I slide into obsession.**

Day 5

Abuse

I stop the cycle of abuse. Emotional unavailability is abuse; it is emotional abuse. When we beat ourselves up, it hurts the whole world. If we beat ourselves up, it makes sense that we will attract someone who abuses us, whether by criticizing us verbally, hurting us physically, or being unavailable. We deserve to know that many people wouldn't even consider yelling when they are angry. Many people wouldn't even consider abusing us or neglecting us. The people in our lives are simply symbols of the way we treat ourselves. In order to heal our partnership issues, we become the partner that we need and want. That means that we are available to ourselves, abstain from self-hatred, and refrain from self-abuse of any kind. If we are experiencing any type of abuse from our partner, we now know that it is not necessary. Bravely searching out the abuser inside of us who is mirrored in our partner helps us to be more loving in our relationship with ourselves, with our partner, and with our world. Today we firmly reject all abusive or neglectful behavior. **Today I do not endure any abuse. I abstain from abusing myself.**

Day 6

Detachment

I detach from the drama. Our society focuses on drama. When our fears of partnership pop up, we love drama because the focus is directed outward.

Because many of us grew up around conflict, we may consider drama exciting. Now we see that drama is exhausting. Love is not a soap opera. Today we detach from all relationship drama because it saps our energy and restricts us from being loving. Although we may have had to cope with drama in the past, and may even feel that we are quite good at it, we know this is the time to let go of conflict. Living without drama seems boring at first and can be very disconcerting for us; however, now we know that inviting calm and serenity into our relationships allows us to enjoy our partner. **I know that I do not need to bring drama into my relationship for excitement.**

Day 7

Manifesting

I manifest my talents. Choosing an emotionally available partner is letting our light shine so that others have the chance to do so too. Reclaiming our talents and manifesting our inner dreams is central to healing. It helps not only us, but a generation of women who can learn what we have to teach and share. One reason our issues with partnership hang on so strongly is that our soul needs to reclaim our precious inner desires. We may have internalized society's ambivalence about women, believing women are less than and need to be taken care of by someone else. Now instead of hiding our light, we express who we are in all our magnificence. In the past, we may have feared shining would turn off or threaten a potential partner. Today, however, we no longer have to worry about others. People are very good at taking care of themselves, and we choose individuals who love to take care of themselves. Empowered people are out there. Let's treat others, and the world, to our shining light. **I see that my partnership issues are friends who will hang on until I begin to manifest my dreams. I let my light shine.**

Day 8

Wounds

I look at my original wounds. We only have two relationships in our lives: our relationship with our mother and our relationship with our father. Whenever we get triggered emotionally in a relationship, it is usually a wonderful indication that some old source of pain in us has risen to the surface. Being triggered does not mean we are not experiencing pain as the result of someone's actions, though; sometimes this is true. People's actions can hurt us; however, if we detach for a while and look closely at the issue, we often see we are experiencing an overly strong reaction to our partner. In this case, it is helpful to move deeper into ourselves and see what our pain relates to. If we were wounded in our family of origin, we may be recreating the struggle with our partner. Or we may have chosen someone like one or both of our parents. Whatever the case, our partnership issues are persistently knocking at our door—encouraging us to unravel our own personal family pain. Today let's make friends with our partnership issues and go deeper into ourselves to uncover, and work out, the original wounding. **I notice when I experience old pain that is triggered by my current relationship.**

Day 9

Reasons

I understand the reason I was in abusive or neglectful relationships. Many reasons kept us in painful past relationships. We may have been naive, needy, recreating difficult family experiences, intensely attracted, or overwhelmed by a person. In order to heal our partnership issues, we need to identify our own personal reasons for choosing to stay in these relationships. The reasons will vary slightly for each of us, yet the essential issue is always the same—an inability to honor who and what we really need in a partner. The process of understanding is not about blame. It is a simple exploration so we can see old patterns that no longer work for us. With knowledge and understanding of our personal reasons for being in painful relationships, we then release these issues. Finally free, we move into relationships that work for us. We enjoy the emotionally available partnership we deserve. **I probe all the reasons I was involved in painful relationships.**

Day 10

Working Out the Reasons

I work out the reasons I was in abusive or neglectful relationships. We need to understand our own reasons for involvement in relationships that didn't work for us. Perhaps a person reminded us of one or both of our parents and we were recreating the struggle, perhaps we looked really good in comparison to our partner with their messy life, perhaps we were rebelling against what our parents or society told us we could have in a partner, or maybe we just got so lonely we took anyone who presented themselves to us. When we know all the reasons, which may be listed here or be a combination of other good reasons, we work to let go of behaviors that no longer serve us. Letting ourselves be with another person before we get too lonely, working out our parental issues, becoming our own authority so we are not rebelling and choosing poorly, and working on our self-esteem are all essential to healing. Today we understand our reasons for being in relationships that didn't work. Then we enjoy an emotionally rich partnership. **I see all the reasons I was in unfulfilling relationships.**

Day 11

Letting All the Reasons Go

I let go of all the reasons I was in abusive or neglectful relationships. To let go of the reasons we were in abusive relationships takes patience and practice. The beliefs that gave rise to our behavior will not disappear overnight; however, understanding our reasons is essential. Delving into our partnership issues gives us a close-up view of why we engaged in behaviors that fostered painful relationships. Whether it was denial, self-hatred, low self-esteem, or just wild attraction which distracted us from the boredom of our own lives, giving up these protections can seem almost impossible. Trusting our process comes in very handy at moments when we are confronted with our reasons for being in abusive relationships. Now we remember that many brave women are walking this path with us. We are not alone. Letting go is possible. Together let's get whatever support we need as we shed what no longer works for us. We do that when we allow the reasons that kept us in painful relationships to be removed and show up for our lives. Letting go is scary, exhilarating, and miraculous. Right now we are doing it! **I am not alone as I release all the reasons that kept me in painful relationships.**

Day 12

Being Trapped

I know that all relationships are open to renegotiation at any time. If we want to get out of a relationship, we sometimes feel ensnared and entrapped. We feel we are being held in an undesirable place. This is an illusion! Many of us were never taught that any relationship is always open to renegotiation. We were usually taught to be good little girls, not powerful adults with the capacity to negotiate for ourselves. As we heal, we may jump into a relationship with a person who doesn't work for us; however, now we know that we are never truly trapped. All relationships are open to renegotiation at any time, for any reason. **I am a rational adult in my relationship.**

Day 13

Taking Ourselves and Our Relationships So Seriously

I wear my relationship like a loose garment. Isn't it boring to be worried about our issues 24/7? All that worry won't help us heal faster or make the relationship work. We must realize we are not powerful enough to influence any situation by being overly serious about it. Everything is being worked out for the highest good. Emotional availability is characterized by light-heartedness. Now we imagine wearing our relationship like a loose garment, rather than constricting clothing. We take some of the pressure off. Talking to others about entertainment, sporting events, the weather, trivia, and news can be an antidote to the dilemma of heavy-heartedness. Our issues are characterized by an obsessive focus on how everything relates to **us**; let's make a choice to get out of ourselves by talking to others. Then we listen to them in return. **I release all over-seriousness.**

Day 14

Getting Away with It

I avoid trying to get away with it. Our partnership issues are about playing the angles, seeing what we can get away with, and other little emotional dishonesties. When we try to get away with whatever we can, it is only a quick fix. The results don't usually last long. Now, whenever we notice ourselves trying to talk ourselves into an attraction we don't feel, or when we start to talk ourselves out of an attraction we do feel, we know we are emotionally shaky. When we try to respond to an inappropriate comment a person makes by ignoring it or skirting the issue of our discomfort, we are trying to get away with something. Living life on life's terms means we actually have to get into the muck of our lives. We have to do some work. We have to let go of control. It may not be as quickly comfortable or convenient to do things the thorough and "effective in the long run" way, but we do get the satisfaction of knowing we have taken the clear path. Healing is about doing the right thing for the right reason. Now we are building a solid foundation for a real relationship that will work. **I do my Higher Power's will and not my own.**

Day 15

Guilt Trips

I abstain from guilt trips. Guilt tripping feels creepy; however, it can be a deeply ingrained behavior in many women. We may think guilt tripping is the only way to get our partner to conform to our wishes. We may have so much rage at people in general that we take perverse pleasure in making our partner feel guilty. Guilt tripping others never works, though. It makes **us** feel bad about ourselves. Often we alienate people completely. Now whenever we have something we need to discuss, we put ourselves in their shoes. Rather than responding from a place of anger when we are tempted to guilt trip someone else, we calm down, imagine how we would want to hear frustration and need from our partner, take a 10 minute time-out, get centered, and then come back and clearly express our needs. Now we refrain from guilt trips. **Today it feels good to avoid guilt tripping my partner.**

Day 16

Man-Eating

I let go of my need to be a man-eater. Man-eating is a good example of partnership issues taken to the extreme. It is a behavior defined by the manipulation of men. It is characterized by lying, stealing, and doing whatever we need to do to get what we need from men. Ultimately, man-eating is a behavior that is unfair to men and women. When all our energy and attention is focused on reeling a man in, we have no energy left for ourselves. Chances are we are stuck when we see him and are only able to think, "Can I get him?" or "What do I need to do to get him?" The panicky need for male attention and validation is so strong sometimes that we eat men up. We are unable to allow for male vulnerability and are inconsiderate of a man's needs. Now we know that whenever we desire to eat a man up, this is the ideal time to move inward. Today we take care of ourselves and our feelings. Man-eating signals that something is out of balance inside of us; and it offers us a great opportunity to figure out what is causing the imbalance. **I notice today when the urge to engage in man-eating kicks up strongly.**

Day 17

Distracting Commitments

I release all distracting commitments. Many women today struggle with doing too much; those of us healing our partnership issues are no exception. As we begin this process, we may notice that we are often compulsively busy. Perhaps one reason we take on distracting commitments is to escape from being truly intimate with another person. If we find that we just don't have time for a relationship, even though we want one, our partnership issues are surfacing. When our actions don't matching our desires, it's time to look behind our distracting commitments. Our busyness interferes with letting an available partner in. What keeps us overcommitted is a fear of saying no to others or wanting to be wanted so desperately. If we notice our busyness detouring us from a relationship we really want, we let go of unnecessary distractions. We are in charge of what we commit to. **I release all busyness.**

Day 18

Paying Attention

I pay attention to myself. Choosing unavailable or abusive partners usually begins early on in women's lives. Then it progresses rapidly. The pattern may ebb and flow as time progresses. Ultimately it may threaten our relationships, our sanity, or our lives. The answer hides behind the symptom, though, persistently waiting for us to notice. Whenever we are involved with, or desire to be involved with, unavailable people, we know that the time has come to pay attention to our soul's message. We are not involved in unfulfilling relationships because we are flawed. We are simply trying to get our own attention. Let's love ourselves today as we hear our own calls to heal our partnership issues. **Today I really listen to myself.**

Day 19

The Hooks

I examine the hooks that lure me in to a person. Why do some people hook us in so strongly, while with other people there is no emotional pull? This may be a mystery for the ages, yet we need to figure out what bait attracts us to the fishhook. We need to freely swim in the sea; however, the hooks are putting us into situations where we can't breathe. The next time we find ourselves hooked in to another person or their drama, we examine what it is about this individual that pulls us in so strongly. Do they possess qualities we admire but feel we lack? Are they like one or both of our parents? Do they try to get our attention? Do they dodge us? Once we clearly see the hook, then we have the chance to truly let go of this type of person. It may hurt a little to get the information. If we are kind to ourselves through the process, though, we get to the other side. As we heal our partnership issues, we no longer go for bait that hurts us. We seek out and are attracted to emotionally available people who give and receive with us. **I unhook from people.**

Day 20

Fulfillment

I sit with the feelings of fulfillment in my body and spirit. Many of us have trouble processing feelings of joy and fulfillment in a relationship. We often want to immediately get rid of any feelings that seem to be "too much." We may be tempted to push someone away or to withhold from them when we feel full of love. We may go to the other extreme, too, and desperately seek to get more attention to prolong the high. We can become a cling-on. Loving emotionally means doing things differently, though. It means sitting with our feelings of fulfillment and truly processing the joy of our satisfaction in love. The quiet, joyful process of healing may be uncomfortable for us. Today, let's remember that love experiences are here to nurture us. Love is not dangerous. Now we honor our ability to be fulfilled with the profound trust that wonderful new love experiences are coming our way. **Today I stay grounded in my feelings of satisfaction with a person I love.**

Day 21

Stubbornness

I release all stubbornness. Bullheadedness keeps us stuck. The definition of insanity is doing the same thing over and over expecting a different result. Whenever we are determined to get what we think we need from a person, our stubbornness traps us. By fighting tooth and nail to get what we want, we alienate others. Stubbornness also manifests in our lives as the tendency to keep coming back to a relationship that doesn't work for us. We convince ourselves we can do things differently to get them to stay, to nurture us, or to love us the way we want them to; however, our job on the planet is not to change another person. Many wonderful, available people want to love us right now. Sometimes our stubbornness prevents us from seeing these emotionally capable individuals. Today we relinquish our need to do the same thing over and over expecting a different result. **Today I try a new way.**

Day 22

Service

I contribute to life. Giving back is our purpose on this planet. Service is not the codependent type of care-taking where we expect to get our needs met by doing things for others. Giving back is contributing to life in order to promote healing for our world. We are powerful beings with a reason for being here. We have a gift to share, even though we may be unaware of it. Actually our relationship struggles are trying to get our attention. Chances are, by the time we are reading this book, we have experienced many relationships that haven't worked out. We wonder how we will ever heal when we haven't found the storybook ending yet. In reality, our search has never been about finding "The One." Our search has been to discover our essence. Many of the people who we have been involved with have symbolized our own challenges to loving naturally. Our interactions with these people, as painful as they may have been, have brought us here where we can finally meet ourselves. Choosing an emotionally available partner is about reclaiming that miraculous power inside us that has a gift to share with the world. The detour to obsessing on relationships has taken us off course from our true purpose, which is to give back. By restoring our true nature, we share ourselves. Then the partner we need appears because we have found ourselves; and they are attracted to **us. I share my gifts with the world in the spirit of service.**

Day 23

Pheromones

I know my attractions are biological as well as emotional. Humans produce and react to pheromones. A pheromone is a scent that each human being emits that alters the behavior of her or his social or sexual partner. The power of smell is undeniable. Scientists say that pheromones are detected by the same nerve cells in the nose used to detect odor. All humans, men and women, emit pheromones at several different sites on their bodies, which is why the way a person smells can be such a turn on. Others are affected by our pheromones as well. They are also affected by an additional scent we produce during ovulation called "copulins," which increases our attractiveness. Now we respect biological attraction as well as emotional attraction, knowing our urges for a person make sense. **I know pheromones elicit non-conscious behavioral reactions in me and my partner.**

Day 24

Willingness

I am willing to release the need to hurt myself. Hurting ourselves is outmoded; however, we may engage in such behavior from time to time because of our deep sense of sorrow. Being with unavailable, neglectful, or even abusive people hurts us. It is painful to constantly seek something that another cannot possibly give to us. The reason that we do this is that injuring ourselves through our choice of partners distracts us from pain we can't identify or can't directly influence. We may feel **something** if we choose someone unavailable, rather than feeling nothing. Hurting ourselves actually makes us feel more in our body rather than so disconnected. As we get better at identifying our emotions, we slowly claim our pain as our truth. We learn to take care of ourselves, love ourselves through the pain, and let go of or modify our connection to what doesn't help us. Today we know that hurting ourselves with unavailable people is unnecessary. Now we bravely relinquish all need to hurt ourselves. We let go of all behavior that does not serve us. **Today I let go of all the ways I hurt myself.**

Day 25

Keeping Up with the Jones's

I abstain from trying to keep up appearances. We are not fooling anyone by trying to pretend things are OK when they are not. And we are not fooled, either. Being perfect and looking good on the outside is highly prized in our society. In order to achieve that, we think we need to be in a relationship. If we are in a relationship, we feel we need to let others think our relationship is good and supportive; however, too often we women take abuse, neglect, or criticism from our partners. Then we try to keep up appearances so people think we are in a successful relationship. It seems safer to want others to like us. As we heal our partnership issues now, we learn that our journey is about **us**. It is an internal journey. If we feel good about our process and our lives, then we will truly shine light out to the world. Healing is about realizing that what others think of us is none of our business. Today we do what we need to do to take care of ourselves. We let go of the "shoulds." Now we love ourselves enough to show the world the wonderful human being inside of us. **Today I let the chips fall where they may.**

Day 26

Scapegoating

I abstain from scapegoating. In our culture we are taught to blame any unhappiness we have on the lack of "that someone special" in our lives. Not being married or in a relationship is a great scapegoat. We blame everything on our lack of a partner. We defer our dreams and happiness until this person appears. We think, "If only I had someone in my life, I would feel good," "I can't have the house of my dreams without a partner," or "If I had a relationship, I would feel better about myself." Using the lack of a relationship as a scapegoat takes **our** power away, though. While waiting for "The One" to come into our lives, we often don't do the necessary footwork to make our dreams happen. And even when we are in a partnership, we often are waiting for that magical moment when everything gels and we feel great forever. Now we see that the solution is not in someone else. If we look closely today as we heal our partnership issues, we see the answer inside of us. **Today I abstain from all blame.**

Day 27

Self-Sabotage

I release the need to sabotage myself. Self-sabotage takes many forms for us. Common manifestations of our self-sabotage include putting other women's needs over our own, fearing we are too old to find a partner, pushing away available people, or engaging in self-hatred. Whatever forms our self-sabotage takes, when we notice ourselves undermining our success, we get clarity. Today we know that any movement to underhanded interference with our own partnership goals signals that our issues have kicked up. If we are self-sabotaging, we are in an uncomfortable situation or experiencing an uncomfortable feeling. Today we thank our desire to self-sabotage with gratitude. Then we gently let go of it. **Today I move into my feelings if I feel the urge to undermine myself.**

Day 28

Mirrors

I practice healthy mirroring. The people we attract are mirrors to us: cold, warm, abusive, loving, critical, fun, and depressive. Sometimes the people in our lives are compilations of all of these traits. If we look closely we see that we are too, for we mirror the individuals in our lives. Our ego wants to separate us from others, yet the qualities we most dislike in others are actually traits that we have in ourselves. If they ignore us, are we ignoring them or ourselves? If they are critical and demanding, do we demand too much from them or from ourselves? If they are warm and loving, are we kind and accepting of them and of ourselves? As we heal our partnership issues, we find that we get back what we put out to either the world or to ourselves. In order to attract the type of person we want in our lives, we need to be that person to ourselves and to others every day. Healthy mirroring begins one step at a time. Today we can do it! **Today I notice the people I am attracting and I look within myself to see if they mirror me.**

Day 29

Twisted Thinking

I release all twisted thinking. Screwy thinking characterizes our partnership issues. Often as we heal, we realize that we have some very twisted ideas of relating. For example, when we meet someone who is available, we may read them as needy. We may think of them as lacking somewhere. We may see their availability as a sign of weakness. Our mixed-up thinking does not comprehend that emotional availability is a source of strength. We don't understand that an available person is open and can let appropriate people in without fear. We may believe that an emotionally available person is not "all there." Our old beliefs tell us that wanting someone results in punishment. We believe that leaving oneself open to a relationship ends in hardships and hurt; however, emotional availability is about love. It is not about punishment and pain. Now when we notice our fears surfacing, we know that the issues are not **theirs**. We know it is **our** twisted thinking in action. **Today, if I am stuck in twisted thinking, I immediately let go of it.**

Day 30

Appearances

I release my appearance obsession around relationships. Looking good at all times with a person assumes a lot of importance in our culture; however, appearances don't always match reality. We want our parents, friends, and neighbors to think well of us. We want others to approve of our choice in a partner. Too often women are taught that the externals are what matter: looks, clothes, job, or car. Externals, however, will not hug us at night and nurture us. Now we turn inward. Today we ask ourselves, "How do I feel in being with this person? How does the inside of this relationship look to me? How does this individual treat me?" When we are clearer about the internal status of our relationship, we are less interested in how our relationship may look to other people. We are more interested in how **we** feel. **Today I release my obsession with appearances in relationships.**

Day 31

Aggression

I notice when I am being aggressive. Aggression is a common trait in women who choose unavailable partners. We may have pursued people when we weren't wanted, may not have been good at taking "no" for an answer, or we may have had a temper. Our angry streak may come out only in intimate relationships.

Women have been taught in our society to be "good" all the time, which often translates to never being mad; however, that anger has gone underground in us. Often we have internalized our anger, becoming depressed or passive aggressive. Unfortunately it has had to come out somewhere. Many of us know only too well that our anger has turned to aggression toward a partner at times in our past. Now we are aware that the key to releasing our tendency to get aggressive is to notice when we feel it starting in us. Whenever we feel we have to **make** them see, to take control, and/or to be the aggressor, we just notice our own behavior. There is no judgment involved in this process. We are getting better and better on this road to healing. Eventually we clearly see that aggression is not necessary, for we know how to meet our own needs. Today when we get angry, we appropriately express it. **Today I know that I do not need to act aggressively with my partner to get my needs met.**

Chapter Summary: Congratulations! At this point you have taken the first steps toward understanding why you push away available partners and tend to gravitate toward those who can't commit. This is the beginning of your journey. It is a solid base to work from.

As you finish this month's messages, ask yourself if you can identify 3 reasons why you tend to choose partners who don't satisfy you. Notice 2 qualities that the unavailable partners from your past have in common. See what behaviors of yours keep you from being intimate with another person.

Right now, the most important thing to remember is that you are not flawed because you engage in this behavior. Women run from intimacy because we fear we don't know how to be in a relationship or because we believe closeness is too scary. In order to heal, awareness must come first. At this point you are on your way. When you understand why you want to run away from those who can meet your needs and why you instead desire to let in people who won't satisfy you in the long term, you are healing. The next chapter deals with the second step, which is simply to observe your behavior without judgment.

·2·

Compassionate

Self-Observation

Chapter 2 teaches self-awareness without judgment. You will learn what does and doesn't work for you in relationships, ways to honor your natural love abilities, and how to keep a sense of loving humor about all of your actions. Move forward with courage! Each day is bringing you closer to an emotionally available partner.

Day 32

Self-Observation

My partnership issues invite me to look beneath my symptoms at the underlying feelings. Whenever our fears take over, we can be certain that there are feelings coming up inside of us. All of our issues with partnership are actually a great tactic we have used to distract ourselves from feelings that seem too painful to face. Our obsessions with unavailable people, detours from intimacy, and anger at those who "did us wrong," are all ways to distract ourselves from feeling the feelings working in us. Many of us have developed this trait to defend against feelings we think will overwhelm us. We fear that if we face our feelings, then nothing will be left. We fear we won't be able to handle the pain; we think that we might die if we feel. Feelings need to be respected, though. We access our feelings by getting centered, meditating, talking to friends, or working with a counselor. Today we have the miraculous opportunity to hear what our feelings are saying, which will heal us. **For this day only, I accept the invitation to look behind my fears at my feelings.**

Day 33

Seeing Our Behavior

I support myself as I clearly see my own issues around partnership. As we see our issues pop up more, we may tend to get hard on ourselves by thinking we are far worse off than we were when we started to heal. It **is** scary

19

to see our behavior so clearly in action; however, if we seem to be pushing potential partners away more, continuing to choose those who are not available, or running from intimacy more, perhaps we are just hyper-aware of how our partnership issues are at work in us. Even if we seem to be acting out more than we did before we started this process, this is the time to be very kind to ourselves on the journey. We are healing and getting better every day, no matter what our behavior seems to indicate. **Today when I see my partnership issues working in me, I trust that I am on the road to healing.**

Day 34

Honesty

I go to the hardware store for hardware. One woman joked: There I go again, going to the hardware store for oranges. Keeping a sense of humor about the allure of people who can't give us what we need is important. Whenever we notice ourselves attracted to someone who is not available, we remember the importance of honesty. Being kind to ourselves, gently questioning our motives if we think we may be trying to "pull the wool over our own eyes," and having a sense of humor about the situation helps. Then we go one step further and ask ourselves what it would be like to be with someone who is available. We deserve a partner who shows up for us. Now we know that looking to unavailable people no longer fulfills us. **Today, with a gentle sense of humor and a big dose of self-love, I remember it is now safe to be with a partner who gives me what I need.**

Day 35

Satisfaction

I ask myself if I am satisfied with a potential partner. We often have no idea what satisfies us in potential partners. We have a fulfillment indicator that is out of order. Many of us are used to accepting the unacceptable in relationships and getting no satisfaction. If this is the case, we may think a lack of satisfaction in relationships is normal. An available person may scare us silly. We find ourselves running the other way whenever someone is eager and available to be with us. Today we know that taking the time to determine our level of satisfaction with an individual is a signal that we are healing. Do we feel calm with an individual? Do we feel empty? Are we comfortable? Choosing an emotionally available partner is about checking in with ourselves to see how we feel around a person, determining that we do feel good in being near them, and then cultivating the ability to let them satisfy us. **I ask myself if someone satisfies me and if I feel good in being around them.**

Day 36

Real Change

I am motivated by a real desire to change. Change is hard, scary, and happens easiest when we are committed to changing. If we are changing for someone else, it probably won't work. If we are trying to change because we think we **should**, we are probably "in for it." If we truly want real, profound change, though, then we will achieve it. Whenever we are in doubt about why we want to change, we get clarity by putting our reasons for wanting to change down on paper or by talking to a trusted friend. Because healing can be arduous, we need to be certain that our motivation is in the correct place. When we truly desire to change, then whatever we do not like about our patterns will be unlearned. Although change may take time, we are steadily healing when our motivation is in the right place. **Today I get clarity about what is motivating me to change.**

Day 37

Investigation

I ask myself if I want to be with this person more, what else I want from them, and if I can stop now. When we love someone, many of us fall into a pattern of giving ourselves over completely to the relationship. Starving for love and connection, we lose touch with our own normal cues of satisfaction. It is a natural tendency to ignore our own stop signals and jump into the love between our partner and ourselves. The reason is that it feels so good. After the glow wanes a little and we feel calmer, however, we may want to get back to our lives. Now, by investigating our own cues of fullness, we learn balance. Then we are better able to love someone else. When we heal, we nurture our ability to be satisfied, both within the relationship and in the world. As we develop sensitivity to our own stop signals, we don't get so close that someone backs away from our neediness. We don't let another person control the relationship, either. Instead, we follow what feels comfortable to **us** in the relationship. We trust that new love experiences and new opportunities for connection are always available for us. **Today I set my own pace in my relationship with a person. I am in balance.**

Day 38

Hormones

I respect my hormones. Hormones can send us reeling. Mental and emotional hormonal effects can include depression, crying spells, anxiety, mood swings, irritability, and withdrawal. Physical symptoms can include bloating, migraine headaches and backaches, changes in sex drives, food cravings, fatigue or insomnia. We can become inexplicably hopeless or madly joyful within minutes. Hormones can make us move away from people or move closer; therefore, hormonal changes are very disconcerting to us and to the person in our lives. Now whenever we get unduly upset with our partner, it is a good idea to check in with where we are in our cycle. Chances are that if we are experiencing especially strong emotions, there is usually a good hormonal reason for it. Often it seems like our relationship is absolutely abominable in such moments. At these times it is important to get a reality check before we make excessive demands on whoever is closest to us. We do not want to lash out at our partner. Obviously we most often are appropriate, and hormones do not always get the best of us; however, our cycles do impact our relationships. **Today I pay attention to my hormones.**

Day 39

Appetite for Love

I give myself patience and time to get my own natural appetite for love back. Being involved with unavailable people gives us very little appetite for love. Although relearning who we are around potential partners, what we need, and what we want may take time, our efforts will pay off. As we heal our partnership issues, getting comfortable with our own appetites for love directs us to the person who is best for us. Today we know that it feels good to regain our appetite for love. Now we ask ourselves questions. Ask, "Do I like to be in relationships fast, or do I prefer to move slowly? How do I feel when I meet someone nice? Do I feel connected right away? Does my desire build slowly? Do I prefer to hold out until I can get the complete treatment or do I like to whet my appetite with appetizers throughout the day?" Letting our desire for a person grow is almost unheard of in our instamatic, "love at first sight" culture. No matter what our relational preferences are, everything we do is just fine. Today we explore what works for **us** in love. **Today I regain my appetite for love.**

Day 40

Mixed Messages

I send clear messages. When we send mixed messages, our partnership issues have flared up. A mixed message takes the shape of saying one thing with our words but doing the exact opposite. Interacting with potential partners gives us the chance to notice when other people give us mixed signals. For example, when a man says he wants a relationship, yet he is juggling several external commitments that keep him busy each night of the week, he is not really available. Interacting with people helps us to notice when they send conflicting signals, but the process also involves noticing our own mixed messages. Like the previous example, are we also too busy for a relationship? There is nothing wrong with sending a mixed message; however, mixed messages can confuse, upset, and alienate other people. When we send mixed messages, the behavior usually indicates that this individual is not right for us, that we are not yet ready for a relationship, or that we are trying to manufacture an attraction we don't feel. Whatever the case, if we notice that the people around us are consistently sending mixed messages; chances are that we are too. **Today I notice if I am sending mixed messages.**

Day 41

Intensity

I decide the intensity level I am comfortable with in relationships. We often jump headfirst into relationships when we are smitten with another person. We forget to keep track of our own boundaries. The relating feels so good, and there are so many fringe benefits from being with a partner, that we are often whisked away by passion. With the tease of a fun relationship, we forget that real partnerships take work; they do not form by magic. Love at first sight does happen; however, being emotionally loving means doing the necessary footwork to build a caring partnership. If we notice that we are obsessing more than usual, feeling abandoned and hopeless when we are not with our partner, or if we are starting to act out compulsively in any other areas, we investigate our intensity level in the relationship. If we notice that we are uncomfortable, it is a great signal to move deeper into ourselves. Now we determine what intensity level works for us. Our partner will not leave us if we take a baby step back; therefore, today we take care of ourselves. **For the next twenty-four hours, I sidestep all extremes.**

Day 42

Acknowledgement

I acknowledge my fear of partnership each step of the way. In order to heal, we need to acknowledge our fear of partnership each step of the way. We often have an unconscious fear of relating intimately. Relationships with unavailable people have hurt and confused us deeply. Chances are that we feel jaded or hopeless by the time we read this book. On a deep level we also know that being with a partner means work, being seen, and showing another person that we are not perfect. This makes taking our part in the emotionally painful relationships we have had challenging. However, only by facing the truth do we have the chance to acknowledge our fears, do the necessary footwork to release these old worries, and love ourselves at the same time. **Today I walk through my fear with self-awareness and compassion.**

Day 43

Old Tapes

I understand all the tapes I have lived with my entire life. Old tapes play over and over in our lives. We may be unaware of how much we are controlled by these recordings. They tell us how to do relationships, what people are legal for us to be involved with, who we are as a partner, and what we should expect of a life-mate. Unfortunately, many of these old tapes are completely out of date. While it may be true that the old tape protected us in the past, this self-protection no longer works. We are not a child or a teenager anymore. Now when we get quiet enough to hear the tape playing, we have the chance to understand the messages. The freedom to let old messages go and record new ones comes from understanding how the old tapes functioned in our lives. At one time, they were necessary, but they are no longer needed. The information is no longer applicable. Today, thanking what kept us safe in the past, we decide that we need healthier messages. By releasing the old recordings, we move on to a wonderful, available partner. **Today I comprehend the messages of my old tapes; I record over them.**

Day 44

Obsessive/Compulsive

I ask myself what I am feeling whenever I obsess, worry, or act compulsively. Beating ourselves up, worrying about aging, diving into self-hatred, and engaging in other compulsive habits are all distractions to keep us from looking at our feelings. Learning to recognize the movement into obsession of any kind helps us see the purpose of our coping mechanisms. Being emotionally shaky is actually a beacon that something is surfacing in us. When we act out, we are either having an uncomfortable feeling or are in an uncomfortable situation. Actually obsession is our friend. Training ourselves to notice a movement into worry, compulsion, or obsession as a call from our deepest power helps us. Often we find that our movement into obsessive/compulsive thoughts makes perfect sense. We use worry to distract ourselves if situations or feelings are too intense. Today we know that when our healing process sends us strongly back to compulsive behaviors we thought we had put to rest, we can get the appropriate professional help we need. Now no matter what pops up, we know we are on our way. We are going to make it! **Today I consider a movement into worry, compulsion, or obsession as a call from my deepest power.**

Day 45

This Special Day

I dedicate this special day to the sacred purpose of getting to know myself. Valentine's Day originated as a marker of the day in February that the birds began to pair. As time passed, the day began to be seen as specially consecrated to lovers. It became a sacred occasion for writing passionate letters and sending tokens of love to the object of affection. Today Valentine's Day can bring up many emotions for women; it's a pretty "loaded" holiday. If we are in a relationship, we may have expectations of what should happen, we may want things to go our way, we may get disappointed, sulk, or pout with our partner. If we are single, we may feel alone, doomed, and hurt; or we may desperately search for a date. No matter what situation we are in, Valentine's Day can stir up a mixture of feelings. This year on Valentine's Day we know we are presented with an opportunity to truly consecrate our love. If we are in a partnership on Valentine's Day, we make it special for our partner and for ourselves by taking in a play or giving each other a massage. If we are single, we plan some extraordinary simple pleasure like dinner with friends or relaxing in a luxurious bubble bath with a good book. No matter what appeals to us this Valentine's Day or what our status around partnership, we love ourselves. We are amazing, miraculous creations who are to be honored. **This year I am my own valentine.**

Day 46

Pursuing People

I discover my natural desires in pursuing others. We get conflicting information about pursuing people. Women's magazines and national bestsellers tell us never to pursue someone. In fact, to spur on someone's interest we are told to pretend to be uninterested or that we are being pursued by a whole slew of people. We often can't "make heads or tails" of all the conflicting messages. Some people assert that they enjoy being pursued by a woman because it takes the pressure off; others say they are turned off by women who pursue them. The question we forget to ask ourselves is what **we** want to do as we interact with potential partners. The truth is that each individual person is unique in their tastes and will respond accordingly. The person who is right for us, and who is right for our relationship style, is out there waiting for us. We only need one good person. If we nurture the wonderful partner inside of us who knows whether she wants to gently pursue an individual, flirt with them, or wait for someone to pursue her, then we attract an available life-mate. **I decide if I want to pursue a person.**

Day 47

Essence

I show safe people my essence. Our essential nature is special and amazing. Unfortunately, we often lead such hectic lives that we aren't in touch with this basic, real part of ourselves. Reconnecting with the wonder of ourselves without fear is a major component of choosing an emotionally available partner. There are many ways to detach from the busyness of the world and explore our essence. Therapy, meditation, writing, inner child work, spiritual seeking, art, dance, and chanting are all great options for getting centered. Whatever avenue we take, we get closer to true love when we get to know ourselves in all of our abundance. By getting quiet and centered, taking the time to explore who and what we are, discovering what we enjoy, and figuring out where we want to go, we find that we are each a treasure. We realize that we deserve to share ourselves with someone who is appropriate for us. Today we know that reconnecting with our own true substance moves us toward the final stage—sharing our Self with a person that we love. **I open myself to my true nature today.**

Day 48

Me

I am clear about who I am. Getting to know ourselves and the fact that we are a great catch is the great gift of healing. That is why our partnership issues are so persistent. A deep magical place inside of us is trying to get our attention to uncover our own magnificence. Being clear about who **we** are then extends to what we want in a partner, what types of people fit well in our lives, what our dreams and goals are, and what we have to give back to the world. Taking into account areas in which we excel, and other places where we may need a little fine-tuning, characterizes self-clarity. Knowledge opens the door to acceptance, and acceptance leads to love. Healing our partnership issues will not hurt us. It will take us on a wonderful journey to honor ourselves. **Today I love the fact that I know who I am.**

Day 49

Success

I am a success. Too often those of us healing our issues connect success with marriage and partnership. We are taught in our culture that "snagging that partner" will make us successful. Success is so much more than a ring on our finger, though. Success means getting up in the morning and lovingly taking care of ourselves throughout our day. Success is doing meaningful work that fills our souls and that is helpful to others. Success is being creative. Marriage and partnership are wonderful; however, these goals may hinder us as we progress in our healing. The reason for this is that we are focusing on a goal that is lauded by society. A wise person once asked: if you knew you would succeed, what would you do? Today we examine what true success means to **us**. Let's note all the ways we are successful right **now**. With a complete willingness to go to any lengths to heal our partnership issues, we **then** create a list of dreams **we** want to successfully accomplish. **Today I see how successful I am.**

Day 50

A Partner

I know what I need in a partner. Chances are we know exactly what we need in a partner; however, we may believe that a person with these qualities does not exist or wouldn't choose us. This is why we are willing to "sacrifice." When we face this dilemma, concrete evidence of our needs supports our healing. We get the facts by writing a list of all the characteristics we want and need in a partner. Then when we connect with a potential partner we take out our list to gently keep us honest. The list reminds us of what we need and what we deserve in a life-mate. It helps us when we may be sliding into relationship with an unavailable person. No one will meet every one of our listed criteria all the time, yet we can trust that there are many stellar people available out there in the world. In fact, one amazing person is waiting for each of us. When we see on paper what we need in a partner and begin to choose individuals who meet most or all of our qualifications, we express and develop these wonderful qualities in ourselves, too. Like attracts like. By being the partner we need, we are attracting an emotionally available partner into our lives. **Today I open myself to awareness of what qualities I need in a life-mate.**

Day 51

My Part

I look at my part in what I do for me.

"What brings you joy?"—Lydia Yinger

Being hard on ourselves, criticizing ourselves, and cutting ourselves no slack are outdated behaviors. We do many wonderful things for ourselves each day. We nourish ourselves with good foods and beverages, we work on our career development, spiritual growth, and physical fitness, and we stimulate our minds with intellectual and cultural pursuits. Many of us expect a partner to fill in the crevices of our lives; however, we may actually be more fulfilled than we think. Resolving our partnership issues encourages us to reclaim what we love in this life, what brings us joy, what we like to do, and who we like to spend our time with. Whether it is creative pursuits like music, painting, or dance; recreational activities like hiking in nature, camping, or mountain climbing; or community involvements such as volunteering, today we make a list of all the nurturing things we do for ourselves. A person gets treated to all that we are when we come into a relationship with them; they are not our source! **Today I reclaim what I love about life. I indulge in what brings me joy.**

Day 52

Messages

I hear the message I am sending myself. We usually have been trying to get our own attention for a lifetime. Denial, fear, and society's messages have often obscured our internal knowledge of who we need; however, the message is strong and repeats itself over and over. Deep down we know what we need in a partner. Paying attention to our own messages is always our antidote to dysfunctional and unfulfilling relationships. Do we enjoy intellectuals, but date athletes instead? Do we yearn for artists, yet only tend to meet business people? Do we feel comfortable with older individuals, yet feel we "should" date people our own age? Today we explore what qualities, interests, and values attract us to a person. Now we really listen to our own messages, for deep down we know who we need. **Today I listen to myself. I hear the message I repeatedly send myself.**

Day 53

Gratification

I ask myself what kind of person will most satisfy me in this moment. Partners are satisfying. People can satisfy us on physical, emotional, spiritual, and sexual levels. It feels good to be with someone who gives to us. In order to figure out whom we will feel satisfied by in any given moment, we must figure out what we need. Asking how we feel helps. Do we need to be held? If so, we ask a nice cuddly person to give us a hug. Do we feel emotionally shaky? If the answer is "yes," then we ask an intuitive and loving individual to hear us as we share our feelings. Do we need a spiritual tune-up? If that is the case, we talk to a priest, rabbi, or another spiritual advisor. Often our partner can meet our needs. If they can't, though, or if we are single, it is OK to get our needs met from other safe people in our lives. Obviously we do not want to make our partner jealous, yet to the extent that it is possible we get satisfied by people today. **I get what I need today.**

Day 54

My Role

I understand my role in my own life. Women have been told what our role is consistently throughout our lives. We have been daughters, students, girlfriends, mothers, caretakers, workers, and employers. Today we expand our definition of ourselves and take into account what our purpose is in our own lives. Much of our issue is about waiting for someone to define, illuminate, and fulfill us. Today we know that we are our own companion. We love ourselves unconditionally, are full of self-trust, and are the catalyst that sees to it that we have every opportunity to reach our own goals. We are our own teacher, healer, lover, parent, child, and employer. We don't **need** a partner anymore; we **choose** to have an individual share our magnificence. **Today I decide what my role is in my own life.**

Day 55

Listening

I listen to myself when I am upset. When we hurt, it is almost second nature to run from the pain. We either run into a relationship with an unavailable person, into obsession, or into some other compulsive behavior. Now when we get upset, we have the opportunity to truly connect within. We get to love ourselves through the experience; however, listening to our feelings can be uncomfortable at first. It may be challenging if we were never taught to go through our feelings without trying to change our emotional state or run from the feelings. As we steadily heal our partnership issues, we learn that feelings do pass. As we take each opportunity to show ourselves our own love, we get to know our true selves. That is a beautiful thing. **Today I just "be" with myself when I am hurting.**

Day 56

Wanting Someone So Badly

I look at my reasons for wanting another person so badly. Every person on this planet, man and woman, has wanted someone badly and lost out. We are not alone. Wanting someone badly is the experience of many women. When we are in this situation, we wonder why they don't want us, we compare ourselves to the people they seem to admire, and we wonder what is wrong with us. Often the problem is that we know very little about a person we badly want. The one we want is merely a projection that we have concocted out of scraps of information. Whenever we experience wanting a person so much, now we stay with ourselves. We ask, "What is it that this person has? What hooks me in to them so strongly? What do I admire in them and feel that I am lacking somewhere?" When we get some clarity about what is going on inside of **us**, we examine if there is any way we can begin to become more like them. This process is about remembering that we are special and amazing, just like everyone else. If another person cannot or will not see our magnificence, then it is time to let go of them. We simply allow our light to shine brightly in another person's direction, and on ourselves. **I get close to myself whenever I want a person so badly.**

Day 57

Knowing Myself

I get to know myself. Knowing ourselves means having a clear vision of our path so that we have an easier time making sense of what we want in a partner. It is essential to our process that we begin to understand what **we** consider non-negotiable in a partner. We can even make another list detailing negotiable qualities that are desirable in a person. Everyone's lists will look different because we all have different tastes and desires. With **our** list in mind, however, we now know that each new experience interacting with an individual is an opportunity to gather more information about what we need.

We search our souls as we interact with potential partners to determine the qualities that will work for us. Now we understand that knowing what we need in another person is not about judgment; it is about self-knowledge. We have power. We are worth all the time and exploration getting to know ourselves takes. Learning what we want in a partner means that we must be fearlessly honest. Today we practice self-exploration with courage. **Today I take the opportunity to figure out what I value in a partner.**

Day 58

Male and Female Views on Sex

I determine what I want from a man sexually. Men most often experience sex as a basic biological need, while women tend to romanticize the sexual act. We usually consider sex as the cementing of our bond with a partner. We think sex will make him want us more. The fact is, though, that often men simply want sex and not a relationship. There is no judgment about the difference in male and female conceptions of sex. A man is not 'bad' if he conceives of sex differently than we do; however, male behavior can wound us if we are not clear about what **we** want from a man. If we want sex from him, that is fine. If that is the case, we must be clear that he may **only** want sex. If we are interested in having a relationship with a man, waiting before sleeping with him is usually a good rule of thumb. Neither way is right or wrong, good or bad. Everything we do is OK. We simply need to be clear on the sexual styles of men and women in order to decide what is good for **us**. **Today I respect the difference in male and female views of sex.**

Day 59

Going Within

I go within right when I feel the craving to obsess on a person. Obsession is the modus operandi of many women who choose the unavailable type. Whenever we beat ourselves up, get jealous, judge ourselves, pigeonhole others, future-trip, decide we can't call a potential partner, read into our interactions with a person, distract ourselves, get bitter, put up walls, or try to get something from another person that they can't or won't give us, we recognize that this is the most opportune time to stop and go within. Getting focused on our obsessions in this way takes practice and perseverance. It is also important to be kind to ourselves as we learn to go inward. The temptation to get hard on ourselves often surfaces when we become aware of how powerful our preoccupations are; however, obsession is the magical opportunity of our partnership issues. Whenever we notice we have slipped into obsession; that is the greatest signal that something uncomfortable is happening, whether it is a feeling we are having or a situation we are in. **Today I go lovingly within as soon as I begin to obsess on another person.**

Chapter Summary: Self-awareness without judgment is a very powerful tool to your healing. When you do a math problem, you don't get upset when you see that 1+1=2. You accept that those are the facts. You may not like the fact that 1+1 doesn't equal 5; however, you simply deal with what is in front of you. You do not judge the numbers! Now, you must look at your behaviors in relationships as if they were math problems. At this point, you are observing many behaviors in yourself which are facts as you heal your partnership issues. You may not like the facts that you are facing, yet you know that judgment doesn't help you. To heal, you must deal with the reality of your part in your relationship struggles, just as if they were facts in a math problem. As this chapter is completed, ask yourself if you now have a better sense of how you use obsession on other people to distract yourself from your life. Notice when you see only what you want to see in potential partners. Be aware when your relationship-related behaviors are affecting your interactions. Right now, the most important thing is to be kind to yourself. If you are seeking out emotionally unavailable partners, you are in good company. Many women struggle with this issue. Pat yourself on the back for your bravery in facing what may be frightening and humbling facts. With the self-observation skills you now have, you are gaining a level of self-understanding that will support you through this journey. You are well on your way. The next chapter will help you love every part of yourself—even the parts you are tempted to judge.

·3·

Being Our Own

Best Friend

This chapter will give you the skills to love every part of yourself. You will learn new ways to nurture yourself, how to believe in yourself more powerfully, and how to have more fun. Enjoy the process of becoming your own best friend. You deserve unconditional love!

Day 60

Pleasure

I please myself. Often women who choose the unavailable type do not have a clear sense of what brings us pleasure. Whether we have been a chameleon deferring to a potential partner's pleasure or are just out of practice in pleasing ourselves, today is the day to explore what we enjoy. Writing a "bliss list" is a great tool. The act of writing all the small pleasures we love to engage in on paper helps us make the decision to do at least one every day. Keeping the "bliss list" handy and placed in our line of sight to have available when we experience challenges is also a great support for us. Some of us may be very skilled already at pleasing ourselves, yet ultimately it is important to remember that we deserve pleasure in our lives just for today. **For the next 24 hours, I surrender to pleasure.**

Day 61

Sustenance

I get support. No matter what issues present themselves to us as we heal our partnership issues, we now face all the challenges with adequate support. Support sustains us on the journey of life. Therapy, meditation, prayer, and service offer much support to us as we heal. Remembering that we are not alone also helps.

Many of us have had to survive without adequate support for decades. This is no longer the case. Today we get the help we need, whether we are single or in a relationship. There are many support groups for women, and we can create a support group dealing specifically with issues of women's emotions if we need it. Also when we are in a partnership, a 12 step program such as RCA (Recovering Couples Anonymous) or a couple's counselor offers support. Another example of support is a connection with other women who are in successful, loving relationships. We have many avenues of support to help us on our way today. We are going to make it! **Today I get all the support I need to heal my partnership issues.**

Day 62

Fun

I take things less seriously. Being overly serious characterizes our fears of partnership. Either there are no people available for us, or we want to escape from all the individuals who do show up. Also, once we realize the extent of our issues, we may work so hard to heal that we lose touch with having a fantastic time. Today let's remember that life is a game to be enjoyed. Let's **have fun**! Our issues are not here to punish us. Our challenges only pop up to get us closer to the wonderful lover inside of us who exults in pleasure and comfort. Whatever relationship we decide to invest in now, we don't have to take it too seriously. Let's enjoy this person in front of us today as we let life happen. **For this day, I enjoy life. I have fun with another person.**

Day 63

Generosity

I am generous with myself. Emotional availability is characterized by a lot of time, intimacy, and an abundance of nurturing and generosity. As we grew up, sometimes our parents weren't generous with their time. They weren't there for us in the ways that we wanted and needed. No parent can always be there for a child, yet today we take back our right to be as generous as possible to ourselves. Generosity means giving freely of our time without any expectation of reward. It means truly loving and caring for ourselves. Whether our generosity takes the form of giving ourselves gifts, playing, connecting with safe people, enjoying some alone-time, or going on a vacation, today we reform ourselves by showering ourselves with love, time, attention, and care. **For this day I treat myself as I would a beloved child.**

Day 64

Pleasing Ourselves

I please myself equally as I please others. Women are very good at taking care of others, and we enjoy pleasing people. Today let's turn that fantastic skill we have honed over a lifetime in toward ourselves. Affirming that we love to give ourselves what we need, this is the time to indulge ourselves in wonderful pleasures. Whether it's taking a bubble bath, lighting a candle, taking a walk, getting a hug, or reading a magazine, we get to please ourselves today. Women who take care of themselves have more to give to the person in their lives, and emotional availability is about giving. Today we know that giving to ourselves will please everyone. Now we indulge ourselves in what pleases us. **I value all of myself. As I give to others, so I give to myself.**

Day 65

Peace

I am at peace with the relationship I have with myself. Choosing unavailable partners is about not loving who we are, judging ourselves, and indulging in self-hatred. For this reason, being at peace with ourselves is imperative to healing. We are acceptable and important. When we love ourselves, our inner peace radiates outward. Loving the self allows us to truly love others. Then we choose those who truly love us back. Does this mean we always love everything we do? No. In fact, emotional availability is about unconditionally accepting everything we do—all the ways we react. Even if we sometimes act inappropriately, have uncomfortable feelings, or overreact, today we accept every part of ourselves. Feeling peaceful means we are internally content. Then we are truly comfortable with another emotionally available person. **For the next 24 hours, I am content with all of myself.**

Day 66

Normal Love

I let myself love normally. What does it mean to love normally? At this point in our process we may feel that we are abnormal and incapable of ever loving normally. We may have been with people who blamed their own issues of being unable to love on us. That is not the truth! We are beings of pure love created by the universe. Our essential natures are love. We only need to return to our original condition.

Today let's look back at all our positive love experiences from the past by writing down at least three examples of times we interacted lovingly with an individual in our relationships. When we concretely see the evidence of our natural love abilities, we realize that we do know how to love normally. No matter how hard we have been on ourselves, how hard others have been on us, or how far off course we seem to have gotten, we do know how to love. By tuning into the part of us that knows what love is, today we release all self-doubt about our love abilities, add successful love skills we see operating in other's relationships to our repertoire, and explore what normal love means to us. **Today I explore what normal love means to me and to others. I let myself love.**

Day 67

Reaching Out

I reach out. Asking for help goes against the grain of many women healing our fears of partnership. We may conceive of needing help as admitting weakness. We also may decide that we should not even bother asking since no one has ever come through for us in the past the way we needed it. Whatever our personal myths about reaching out for comfort and assurance, today we re-conceptualize asking for help. In actuality, whenever we reach out to others we give them a gift that says, "I trust you." "I need what you have to give me." Also, if we reach out, we are capable of being available when others reach out to us. Not everyone will be available when we reach out; however, we can practice the new behavior. Through that we learn who is available. By reaching out to safe others we widen our support network, too. This is important because a good support system is essential to a healthy partnership. Since no one person can meet all our needs, now we get the support we need in a variety of ways. Today we let others love us. **Today I ask for comfort and assurance from supportive people.**

Self-Protection

I protect myself from harm. Healing means knowing what harms us. Every woman will be slightly different. We are responsible for ourselves as adult women, and identifying who is harmful for us is important. Growing up we may have been in experiences where those we depended on were unsafe; sometimes they were even dangerous. We may also have been in relationships with people who, for whatever reason and on whatever level, were not safe partners. Even if we are used to danger and discomfort, as adults we now can choose who we let into our lives. With self-knowledge of what is harmful for us, we seek out the plentitude of potential partners who are safe and less painful for us.

Healing our partnership issues offers us a great daily opportunity to get very good at keeping ourselves from harm. Now we know who and what to avoid as we let our experience guide our path. We also have abundant resources to learn how to protect ourselves from harm, including self-defense classes. (See the Bibliography at the back of this book.) No matter what path we take to protect ourselves, today we know that we deserve to be with people who are safe. The beauty of it is that safe individuals are everywhere! **Today I learn self-protection skills.**

Day 69

The Bottom Line

I accept and love myself no matter what. There are many bumps on this "wild ride" of healing. We are unlearning patterns of behavior that took a lifetime to develop. We will appear to "fail" several times; therefore, being unconditionally loving of ourselves sets a profound energy in motion when we "slip." Eventually we get so good at unconditionally accepting ourselves that we know how to give love and acceptance like this to a partner as well. As we make progress, we see that the love we give ourselves is reflected back to us by others. Whatever happens on our journey, we are precious, valuable, and special. We deserve to give ourselves all the love and caring we can muster. Whatever types of behavior we exhibit and whatever we do, we are always acceptable. Even though we may not like our behavior, we are wonderful, loving beings. For help, we only need to turn inward. We are going to make it. Though this process often takes time, we will not fail if we practice day by day. **Today I love myself no matter what.**

Day 70

The Truth

I tell the truth.

"To thine own self be true."—William Shakespeare

Loving an available partner is about being true to ourselves. It is having the courage to appropriately share our truth with people. Taking responsibility for our own truth presents a real challenge for many of us. Because we were involved with unavailable people, we remember many times that our honesty was invalidated by others. In the past, speaking with candor drove significant people away. Today as we move toward emotionally available partners, we learn which people are safe to share intimately with. With persistence and practice day by day, we begin to associate integrity with intimacy and connection. Now we know that we are protected when we take risks to share ourselves. Practice in every interaction we undertake also teaches us how to express our truth successfully. Now we courageously make a decision to practice speaking with frankness as we go through each day. We can do it! **For this day only, I speak what's true.**

Day 71

My Best Friend

I am my own best friend. If we had a friend who talked to us the way we talk to ourselves, chances are that person would never be in our lives; however, in intimate relationships with others we often accept unacceptable behavior. We sometimes subject ourselves to criticism, abuse, and control—probably because we are treating ourselves the same way. If we are used to coping with our own abusive self talk, then it makes sense that we would attract and be attracted to those who are not truly our friends either. Today we define what a best friend is to us; then we strive to become that best friend to ourselves. In time we are unable to be with an unavailable person. We can't because we would never let our best friend be hurt. **Today I love**

every aspect of myself. I am friendly and kind to myself.

Day 72

Utility

I use my relationship as a way to grow and share. Relationships are a great way to learn about ourselves and others. In fact, many people believe that we are not growing as much as we can unless we are in a relationship. This produces a quandary for many of us. We are aware that relationships are fertile ground to work through our issues. We do want to share ourselves in relationship, yet our fears of intimacy make us shy away from what can be good for us. When we see ourselves with such clarity, it is important to truly love ourselves and trust our process. The next relationship we have or the next interaction we have with our current partner will never be as painful as the interactions we have had before. Now we are moving forward on a path to true healing and acceptance. We are getting better every day. Today we know that we deserve the chance to utilize a relationship to promote our growth, and the growth of our partner. Now we move forward with courage. **Today I move into a relationship in order to heal.**

Day 73

Touch

I take care to avoid touch deprivation.

"Right now massage is filling a need for me."—Diane

The lack of touch in a woman's life can create a vast ache. Touch deprivation can lead to fear. It may even make us connect with unavailable or inappropriate people just to quiet our needs. It is always OK to be with any person that we choose; however, now we remember that we deserve to be with someone who shows up for us. We deserve to get our needs for appropriate touch met, too. When touch deprivation issues surface in our process, massage can be extremely healing. If we can afford it, we indulge in sensual, appropriate touch. We can hire a massage therapist, get a friend to gently give us a foot rub, take a massage course and learn to self-massage, or trade massage with a safe individual. We can also get a nurturing hug from someone who cares about us. Today there are ways for us to get our needs met safely and appropriately as we heal. Now we go to any lengths to take care of our Self. **Today, I know how to get my needs for touch met.**

Day 74

I Deserve

I am entitled to love, respect and honesty. Love is characterized by respect and honesty. We deserve to be treated with love and care. Respectful, honest people are out there waiting for us. If we are currently choosing relationships with those who are not loving and caring, we examine the connection binding us to someone who is not right for us. When we check in with ourselves, we clearly see that staying in relationships with unavailable people is a manifestation of **our** partnership issues. It is always OK to be with someone who cannot give us what we need; the important thing is to notice. No matter where we are, today with great self-compassion we take the next right steps. We affirm our right to be treated with love. Then we open ourselves to an emotionally available partner. **Today I know that I deserve love.**

Day 75

Acting Out

I get a chance to learn about myself whenever I act out. Let's face it, change is scary. If we do something that doesn't meet our own standards, chances are that we are in good company. Whenever we act out, that is usually a good indication that we are in an uncomfortable position or are experiencing a feeling we can't deal with. Emotional behavior is normal as we heal our partnership issues, and even necessary. It may not feel good in the moment; however, it means that we are changing.

As we heal, we learn that "less-than-nurturing" behavior is actually a positive experience. We learn from the experience with humility, acceptance, self-love, and a desire to do better next time. If the process is not always smooth, all we need to do is love ourselves. Looking more closely at our behavior and remembering that we are not alone helps us see that our acting out has a precious message for us. We get to experience how painful it is to "act out." Then we can change our behavior. No matter what we do, the words "I'm sorry" are very healing when accompanied by a sincere change in behavior. Today we learn from our actions as we heal our partnership issues. **If I find** myself acting out today, I learn from it.

Day 76

Focus

I refocus my course today. There are times when we will get off course in this journey. Painful world events, boredom, loneliness, and desire can all serve to hook us into someone who cannot be what we need. At these times, it is essential to stop and get clarity about our true goals for a relationship. When life becomes too much and our direction becomes hazy, the desire to connect with an unavailable person may become incredibly strong. In these moments, we must refocus on our true desire, which is to heal. If we feel we are getting shaky, distracted, or off the beam, today we get centered once again. Fun, friends, a support group, therapy, meditation, dance, art, writing, and prayer are all tools to help us get back on track. Now we know that we are worth the effort! **Today I support myself if I notice I am veering off course toward a person who cannot give me what I need.**

Day 77

Compassion

I develop compassion for myself. Feelings are very scary for many of us. Growing up, we may not have seen adults who were able to handle and process their emotions. If this was the case, we deduced that feelings were too scary to face. In a variety of ways, we learned to escape from our feelings. Being in relationship with unavailable people seems like a great escape. Then the risk of truly getting close and getting hurt is impossible. Today, however, our protection from getting hurt is stifling us. Now we clearly understand the reasons why we needed to escape our feelings. With great courage, we release our old protections. Then we develop compassion for ourselves which helps us overcome our relationship challenges. Compassion comes from understanding all of our lives: childhood, adolescence, and adulthood. As we practice compassion for all the experiences that have made us who we are today, we spontaneously respond to ourselves in order to heal our partnership issues. **Today I view myself with love.**

Day 78

Female Sexuality

I honor and trust my own sexuality and femininity. Women's sexuality has been villainized for centuries. Starting with the story of Adam and Eve, temptation has done us in. Being a sexual woman in our culture still raises taboos, even in this new millennium. Today we know that part of healing means reclaiming our own sexuality and femininity. We do this by honoring our sexuality, even if our relationships with sex have been tangled. Allowing our own bodies, minds, and souls to direct our sexual activity teaches us that our sexuality is magical, good, pure, and profound. Obviously we do not want to expose ourselves to disease. We also may not want to have sex indiscriminately; however, we can have sex any time we want to. It is always OK to have sex when the time is right. If we want to wait, that is a great method of letting our Self signal when we feel comfortable having sex. Getting to know a potential partner gives us the added bonus of feeling our own desire for them mount. Whatever avenue we take with another person today, everything we do is acceptable. We honor ourselves by reclaiming our sexuality. **Today I love and honor my sexuality.**

Day 79

Emotional Hangovers

I take care of myself whenever I experience an emotional hangover. Emotional hangovers do not feel good. They lead to aches and pains in the body, lack of focus in other areas of our lives, and emotional depression. Whenever we act inappropriately or with less skill than we would like in the relationship arena, we may experience a hangover. Emotional hangovers hurt. We tend to blame ourselves. We mull over the problem again and again. There are many situations that crop up on this journey that may lead to an emotional hangover: relationships that aren't working, interactions with people that remind us of our early love experiences, seeing our ineffective patterns clearly in our behavior, being rejected, being pursued, or feeling old wounds pop up. The cure for any hangover is always the same. To recover from an emotional hangover, we wait it out, note that we feel bad, and know that it will pass. Eventually we experience freedom when we move on to people and behaviors that do not lead us to emotional hangovers. **Today I**

abstain from behaviors and from people that leave me with an
emotional hangover.

Day 80

Adequacy

I am already good enough to sustain a wonderful relationship.
Sometimes we are hard on ourselves. Women mostly believe that if we just
work harder, do more, and act right, then we will someday be good enough
for a great relationship. In truth we don't have to work so hard to be loved
and valued. There is a wonderful partner inside of us who already knows how
to love ourselves and another person well. This internal partner is waiting
patiently for us to believe we can give love successfully.

Our healing process gets us closer to the being within us who knows how to
love. We do this by shedding all the behaviors we have gathered in fear and
panic, and from various cultural and parental sources, throughout our
lifetimes. We practice interacting with potential partners, we check in with our
feelings when we are with an individual, we determine who feels good to us,
and we figure out what qualities are essential for us in a life-mate. Then we
access the partner we are seeking; she is inside of us patiently waiting for us to
free her. Now by giving our Self a chance to love, we love every part of
ourselves. **Today I know that I am adequate to maintain a loving
relationship.**

Day 81

Whatever It Takes

I do whatever it takes to give myself who and what I really need. Self-
care is the part of adulthood that is so appealing. We have power available to
us to take care of ourselves today. Whatever our partnership status, we do all
the necessary footwork to get where we want to go. No matter what our
relationship situation, we now do whatever it takes to give ourselves who we
want. Any status around partnership allows us to explore how a person can
meet our needs. When we are in a partnership, we get concrete experience in
what works for us with a person, we practice asking for what we need, and we
experience the day to day process of relating. Being single also makes it very
opportune to give to ourselves. We use dating and interactions with a variety

of people as a good way to figure out what qualities we need in a partner, what types of individuals work for us, and to practice loving ourselves unconditionally. We are important and deserve to indulge in self-care. **Today I go to any lengths to meet my own needs.**

Day 82

Laughter

I laugh to heal myself.

"Laughter is the only medicine with no negative side effects."—Anonymous

Laughter feels good. It connects us to that loving, playful child within us. When we are healing, it can be hard to laugh. Having fun can be challenging. As we heal, we often realize that it may have been a long time since we laughed out loud. This happens because we are so focused on getting better. Today we know that we can do something to make ourselves laugh. Whether we see a silly movie, host a games night party at our house, or go to the comedy club, getting ourselves laughing is balm to our spirit as we work through our partnership issues. The pay-off is a release from the seriousness that keeps us stuck. Then we are able to have fun with an emotionally available partner. **Today I laugh with pleasure at the sheer joy of life.**

Day 83

Support

I support myself as I learn from my mistakes. Everyone makes mistakes. That is just part of life. Mistakes are usually food for regret; however, regret is a slippery place for us. Now if we are open to learning from our mistakes, we see that mistakes aren't "bad." In fact, mistakes actually have the magical power to teach us lessons. We want to be healed, or we wouldn't be reading this book. For this reason, today we look at our "mistakes" as learning experiences. With self-support, we experience the hurt our "mistakes" have caused us. Then, when we have the information that something doesn't work for us, we change. Healing is about information not judgment. Now we no longer judge ourselves. We know that reframing "mistakes" is the most compassionate way to support ourselves. Today we respect and learn from our "mistakes." **I honor myself and my "mistakes" today.**

Self-Care

I ask myself what I need and what do I can do for myself. Questioning ourselves gently about what we need assumes that we can answer. Then we are able to act lovingly to take care of ourselves. Often we think in extremes, though. We think that someone else will provide the fairy tale for us or that no one will ever give anything to us. We think, "What's the point in asking?"

The process of reclaiming the natural lover inside of us means that we become **our** own loving partner. Today we develop the skills to use all our magnificent power to fulfill our needs and desires. First, we ask ourselves what we need. Next, we respond by focusing on our needs. Slowly and magically, with consistent practice, we then are able to share our needs with a person. With daily experience, we get our needs met. **Today I possess excellent self-care skills. I gently ask myself what I need.**

Day 85

Self-Treatment

I treat myself with love, care, and attention. Our partnership issues have often inhibited us from treating ourselves well; however, we are now learning that good self-treatment feels wonderful. We see the evidence that meeting all our needs as soon as humanly possible reaps real rewards. Our excellent self-care skills help us to love, care for, and pay attention to ourselves as well as to a partner. Getting better acquainted with our needs and learning to lovingly respond to ourselves, we have less **need** for a partner and more ability to **accept** love. Ultimately our relationships have a real chance for growth and sustenance now. Today we eagerly practice self-love and good self-treatment in order to give ourselves the gift of an emotionally available partner. **Today I treat myself well knowing I can treat another person equally as well.**

Day 86

Giving

I give myself exactly who and what I want. Our fears pop up when we have faith only in ourselves. We are frightened when we find we are incapable of manifesting an emotionally available person; however, the good news is that the universe wants to give us who we need. Even though we don't have the power to manifest our ideal mate, an emotionally available person is out there waiting for us.

Right now we can be around those who are ideal for us. We deserve to be with the people we want. If we decide we like professional individuals, then we join a professional society to attend lectures and social events. If we become aware that we like sporting people, we explore recreational activities. If we like artists, we explore our own creativity through classes or creative pursuits. It is important to remember that as women we have choices about those we spend our time with. Now we give ourselves exactly who and what we need, whenever we need it. Obviously we need someone else's permission for this, yet we indulge ourselves to the extent that it is possible. Even if giving ourselves the person we need takes the shape of going to see a play or movie with our favorite actor, we are getting closer to that person in real life by examining who and what we want in a partner. **Today I indulge myself by surrounding myself with those I enjoy.**

Day 87

Compliments

I take in a person's compliments. Women healing our fears of partnership often have a hard time believing it when someone appreciates us. We are often tempted to think, "What is wrong with them?" Or we may wonder why they didn't also include all our other wonderful characteristics in their compliment. It may seem as if a person can do nothing right around us with compliments. This is usually a persistent signal that we are stuck. To say, "No, I'm not really that attractive, talented, special, or accomplished" or "I am the best," makes a person wonder. A compliment is a gift from another person. Today we choose to let that gift in rather than rejecting it. Even if it is hard to hear a compliment, saying "Thank you" when someone compliments us is a sufficient response. We do not need to immediately compliment them back. Instead let's actually cherish the gift of a compliment. Let's allow it to feed our souls. **Today I love to be showered with compliments.**

Security

I am secure in my love. Although security feels good, consistency and stability were often missing from our past relationships. We rarely felt safe and secure because of our fears. Our choice of unavailable people made our lives unstable, too. Chances are that now as we heal our fears of partnership, we envision love as void of security. We may be terrified to form warm, tender, affectionate personal attachments today.

Love itself is the antidote to fear, though. Now we cultivate freedom from danger in our lives. We begin by loving ourselves and keeping ourselves safe. Now whether we set boundaries or take a self-defense class, we realize we are precious. We do whatever it takes to keep ourselves safe. Getting grounded in the love we have for ourselves then creates a self-assurance that guarantees us safety. With time and practice, that self-love extends—it grows into the ability to truly give love to others. Now we love because we know that what we give, we get back. **I safely love with tenderness and affection.**

Day 89

Showing Up

I show up for myself over and over. "Whatever it takes" is the motto of women committed to choosing an emotionally available partner. Some of us will progress quickly in certain areas, yet find that our process is challenged in other places. For example, we may become good at connecting with our feelings, but continue to obsess on unavailable people. Others of us may find that we are easily attracted to available people; however, we experience real difficulty in sharing intimately with our partner once we are in a relationship.

Whatever challenges we face, trust the process. The journey can be long. This is because it takes practice and patience to learn and implement new behaviors. Even though we may get discouraged, we are excellent at not giving up. We will heal. The progress may even happen quickly! As long as we persevere and trust in all our self-growth, our work pays off. The relationship issues may even become less important as we enjoy the true love of being available to ourselves. **Today I show up for myself. I know that I am on this path for as long as it takes.**

Day 90

Status

I love myself no matter what my status. Married, single, in a relationship, or not; we love ourselves no matter what. The status symbol of being with a partner is almost a cultural obsession today. The relationship status quo makes it easy for us to feel "less than" whenever we are not in a relationship. We may wonder when it will happen for us. We are tempted to believe that finding the "right" person will mean that the struggle is over. For many of us, our focus needs to be directed inward not outward. Self-love is what we are really searching for. It is wonderful to be loved and appreciated by another person; however, the true gift of love is profoundly loving and accepting ourselves right now. **For the next 24 hours, I know that my status depends on how much I love myself.**

Chapter Summary: Self-love and self-care feel good. When you shower yourself with love and good treatment, you learn that you deserve. Then when you meet a potential partner who treats you poorly, you don't get "hooked" on them. Your radar has changed. You are attracted to more emotionally present people.

At this point, you are more used to being loved well. Emotionally available partners are starting to look more interesting. This is a process, though. It takes time. You have been hurting for a while now in relationships. To heal, you must consistently practice self-care to let kind people in. If you find you are still attracted to emotionally unavailable people, this is normal. At this stage, all you need to do is persevere.

Right now, choose 3 self-care behaviors from this chapter that you can do each week. Write a list of 10 activities you find pleasurable. Pick 1 item from your list to try out. Schedule some time for fun. You are worth all the work this takes.

The next chapter on building your confidence will take a lot of courage, so having fun sets the foundation for the next powerful step. Now you are ready for some magic tools that will help you kiss the unavailable type goodbye forever!

·4·

Magic Tools That

Build Confidence

Chapter 4 offers you a variety of confidence-building strategies. You will become skilled at setting boundaries, at improving your communication skills, and at discovering what you really need in a partner. As you read this chapter, note some tools that you would like to try out. Then practice. As soon as you feel more confident about yourself, you will be ready to share love with an emotionally available partner.

Day 91

Setting Boundaries

I set boundaries. Although setting limits is often a new experience for women, boundaries are useful tools that protect us. An example of a boundary is when one woman told her partner that she was not available to take calls after 10pm. When she clearly defined where she began and ended, everyone benefited. Her partner was happy to call her before her cut-off time. Like her, we help others when we set boundaries. People want us to feel comfortable. The limits we set protect us from second guessing, too. Then we don't wish we had done something different.

The stumbling blocks to boundaries only pop up when we expect another person to respect our boundary while we ourselves do not. For example, another woman told her new romantic interest that she was working on a project and wouldn't be able to talk to him via the telephone for two weeks. Then one night **she** called him. Happy to hear from her, he responded. They talked for a long time and the woman later blamed the incident on him. This is not OK. Along with setting boundaries comes the added responsibility of maintaining our own boundaries. If we decide we want to re-negotiate a boundary with our partner that is always fine; however, we ourselves must do the work to initiate the boundary's renegotiation with someone. This woman's solution was to call him and say, "I miss you, but I can only talk for five minutes." He was happy to respect her limit. Today we take responsibility for ourselves within the partnership by setting and re-negotiating boundaries. **Today I set limits in my relationship.**

Day 92

Communication

I have the skills to tell my partner what is up. Even though women are trained in our culture to be effective communicators, we may feel we missed some essential classes preparing us for communicating in intimate relationships. The fact is that we need to evaluate our own skill level in communicating with others. We may lack some essential relationship skills, we may be trying to communicate with someone incapable of hearing us, or our timing may be off. Whatever the glitch, when we have gathered significant information about our present abilities in intimate communication, we affirm that where we are today is just fine. From this place of acceptance, we observe what works for other women; perhaps add some new methods to our skill set, and practice! (See the Bibliography for resources on improving communication.) **Practice makes perfect. Today I know that I possess all the skills I need to communicate effectively with my partner.**

Day 93

Self-Talk

I tell my inner child that she is precious The inner child in us needs a loving parent. She is playful, bright, adorable, precious, vulnerable, and loving. Many of us had to struggle to survive when we were children. We may have had familial or financial crises to deal with as we grew up. Because we were dealing with more pressing problems, we didn't often daydream about partnership. Today, however, we are adults who are safe. We can now daydream about what we want in a partner. We also have the honor of self-parenting with care. We can get closer to that small, sacred part of us by connecting lovingly with our inner child. Self-talk is a wonderful tool to connect with this special part of ourselves. As we get closer to that tender part of us, we are no longer able to expose her to relationships that are unsatisfying and often even harmful. She knows exactly who and what she needs in a partner. She is waiting patiently to tell us. When we have a strong dialogue going with the child inside us, then we are connected with that still, small, honest part of us—the child inside. **I shower my inner child with love, attention, and care.**

Day 94

Meditation

I sit quietly and meditate. The daily practice of meditation helps us connect to the power of love in the universe. By getting quiet and still, we get closer to our own wisdom—the wisdom deep inside of us. Meditation is practiced in many ways. For beginners it is good to have a teacher to help guide us. Meditation teachers can be found in the local phone book or on the internet. As we practice meditation, we learn that many thoughts float in and out of our minds all the time. We find that the chance to sit quietly and pay attention is invaluable. The most important thing is to not get distracted by the thoughts coming and going. When we notice ourselves thinking, we gently return our focus to the breath or to another steady rhythm such as a mantra repeated over and over. Meditating with a group is good. Meditating with a partner is a wonderful experience as well. Also, meditation has several benefits: it helps us to get grounded in love before speaking with our partner when we have been challenged in our relationship, it keeps us looking years younger when practiced consistently, and it helps us to love ourselves more powerfully. Whatever way we engage in meditation, the practice itself heals us. **Today I practice meditation for fun.**

Day 95

Humor

I maintain a sense of humor. Keeping a sense of humor is perhaps the most important ingredient to our success. We may experience a lot of pain as we look at all the reasons for our difficult relationships, and interact with potential partners in new ways which are uncomfortable for us. Our humor can lift us out of the challenges with partnership, though. Humor helps us remember that "this too shall pass." Laughter is the best medicine. Playful, gentle humor works wonders. Today let's remember that we are not alone in this process. Many brave women are healing. With a wonderful sense of humor about our journey, we are healing too! **I let my sense of humor pull me through.**

Day 96

Discriminating Wisdom

I discriminate wisely with potential partners. Discriminating Wisdom is a Buddhist term that describes the recovery of our own inherent wisdom. It is an opportunity to discriminate and decide who is right for us. The key elements in Discriminating Wisdom are our intentions. Intention fixes the mind on some purpose or goal with a person. Our intention initiates our verbal and physical actions. When our intention is supported by the attitude of love, rather than the attitude of manipulation, then we discriminate wisely with people. New intentions with people arise all the time, though, so the only way we give our lives direction is through Discriminating Wisdom. When we know the actions that lead to happy experiences with others and the pitfalls of behavior that will lead to our unhappiness, then we are open to an emotionally available individual. Every interaction we have with potential partners lets us watch for the intention behind our action. As we interact, we see the effect it has on our relationship. Today freedom from suffering in relationships means that we act with love, compassion, and wisdom for ourselves and for our partner. Now we discriminate wisely. **I use Discriminating Wisdom to make my relationship choices today.**

Day 97

Stop Signals

I listen to my own answers and stop. Emotional availability knows there will always be a new love experience waiting to refill us when we need it. Love is everything; the whole universe is love. Love doesn't just come from our partner. We have much love to give as well as to receive; however, our partnership issues make us want to hoard. We think we need to get as much as we can in relationships as fast as possible. We are afraid to let go of another person. We fear we may not ever be as full of love for them again as we are right now. When we are full of love for our partner, it takes great courage to stop and let go a little. With practice, though, we see that stopping when we are full allows us more opportunities to experience our desires.

Taking a baby step back from our love lets us refill ourselves anytime. Then we experience the magic of feeling our desire well up! Today we heed our own stop signals for fun and pleasure. **I know there will be a fresh new love experience waiting for me as soon as I feel desire for my partner surface again.**

Day 98

Attraction

I can attract a wonderful, loving, non-abusive, available partner. Believing we deserve a wonderful person in our lives is often the most challenging part of healing our partnership issues. Most people have to deal with raising their low self-esteem. We are no exception. When we choose an unavailable partner, we are being signaled that we do not feel deserving. In order to raise our self-esteem, many women on our journey have found self-hypnotism, written affirmations, prayer, and meditation effective methods for believing that we can attract an available life-mate. The next step, which may be even more challenging, entails believing that we can be attracted to, can want, and are ready to let in a loving, wonderful, and non-abusive partner. No matter how hard it is, now we reform our beliefs. As soon as we believe we are ready for a wonderful individual, the universe creates the circumstances so that they appear in our lives. Today we know that this is the perfect day to affirm our desire for an available person. **Today I am eager and ready to accept a wonderful person in my life.**

Day 99

Speaking Up

I am active about speaking up when I have something to say. Speak up! Say what you feel! Ask for what you need! Too often women in our society are told to keep silent about our needs, feelings, and opinions. Not speaking up often leaves other people frustrated and guessing, though. When they guess wrong, everyone is unhappy. People aren't mind readers; it is unfair to expect them to know what we need. Emotional availability is about speaking up and letting the other person see who we are when we are unsure of the response. Our needs won't always be met when we have something to say; however, today we take the risk of speaking up. We courageously let another person see us. **For today I actively speak up if I have something to say.**

Day 100

Wish Lists

I honor my list of the qualities I need in a partner.

"Any lawyer in this town will tell you he meets every one of your criteria in a partner."—Marilyn

Women often have a wish list of the partner we want. We crave the status symbols associated with relationships: the fine house, the two incomes, and the 1.5 children. It is good to have a list of what we want in a partner; however, we may be disappointed if we expect to get all of it, all the time, from any one person. That's why creating a list of all the characteristics we consider non-negotiable in a person is vital to healing. Examples include being unattached, being honest, and being financially stable. A list of "negotiables" (whatever we want in a partner, yet isn't essential) can also be helpful. Using these lists when dating or when in relationships assists us in seeing if a person meets our criteria. In the end, though, we know that no one can meet all of them all the time. As we progress with an individual, we discern what we can live with in our partner with fearless honesty. Sometimes we use an objective helper like a trusted friend or therapist to get clarity. Then, even more importantly, we strive to be the person on our lists—because like attracts like. **Today I honor my lists of "non-negotiables" and "negotiables" when I am with a potential partner.**

Day 101

Enmeshment

I unwrap and untwist from my partner. Enmeshment is like being ensnared in a net, tangled and helpless. Now whenever we are tempted to intertwine with our partner, we realize we are not taking care of our own lives. Unhooking from our partner gives us the chance to tend to ourselves. We trust our partner to manage their own affairs; however, when we see our partner in pain it is natural to want to help them. This is where the process of healing has an important lesson for us. Our healing teaches us that although it may look like our solutions will help our partner, our ways most often do not work. Today we know that trusting others to figure out what they need allows us to unwrap and untwist from our partner. Detachment enables us to truly be helpful to ourselves and to someone we love. Now we make a decision not enmesh with our partner. **Today I let go. I keep the focus on myself.**

Day 102

Needs

I can get what I need from people. Opening up to an emotionally available partner means sharing ourselves and our vulnerabilities. We do this when safe sharing is appropriate. Because we often associate needing with neediness, though, letting people know that we have needs can be scary. What many of us forget is that relationships are about give and take. When we believe we can get our needs met, we ask for what we need. Then we see that many people are capable of meeting our needs. If we don't ask, we definitely won't get our needs met. Appropriately asking for others to help meet our needs benefits others too. When we ask for help, it gives others the power to help us. People have a lot of offer us; human beings are infinitely rich. Now we learn that letting other people in takes practice and courage, but we get better every time we reach out for help. **Today I get what I need from people.**

Day 103

Passion

I find and express my creative passions. Part of the desire to find "The One" is to give our lives meaning. We may believe that a partner will give us a purpose, children, a home, and a dog. In the meantime, though, we are forgetting our amazing, miraculous, spiritual abilities. We lose sight of the fact that we have a reason for being on this planet. In our society it is easy to get distracted from what brings us alive. We are all encouraged by cultural mores to follow the rules and play the game. Women are particularly targeted if we don't conform to society's expectations; however, now we know that our creativity **also** needs to come out. We are passionate, creative individuals who have something to say that our world desperately needs to hear. Our relationship challenges will hold on until we figure out our purpose. The issues will pop up until we reclaim our creativity and passion. Now we know that expressing ourselves is what this work is all about. We search for **our**

light. **I am creative and passionate right now, with or without a partner.**

Day 104

Energy

I keep my energetic boundaries. Women's energy is precious. In fact, energy equals power. When people want our attention, when we feel stared at, and when we sense that others want to feed off our energy, we have the opportunity to maintain our own power. Now we no longer give it away indiscriminately. As we heal, we learn that simple, unobtrusive postures contain energy that we do not want to give away. Crossing our legs at the ankle, putting our hands together with the thumbs touching, and imagining ourselves surrounded by an invisible shield are all ways to appropriately maintain our energy. Today we decide who we share our power with. We keep our energetic boundaries. **I contain my energy if I want to.**

Day 105

Gratitude

I practice gratitude.

"Whenever I get really upset, as soon as I calm down a little, I get out a sheet of paper and write a list of all the blessings in my life. I am usually amazed by how long it is."—Luisa

Whenever we feel down we can quickly make a list of all the blessings in our lives. Friends, the chance to heal, having all our limbs intact, the opportunity to listen to our partnership issues, the ability to hear what these issues are telling us, and indoor plumbing are just a few ideas to begin. It is a pleasurable experience to generate a gratitude list about how lucky we are to be living right now in this moment. Whenever we feel down, gratitude takes us off the "pity pot." It put us on the road to true healing. Also gratitude feels good. Anytime pain threatens to overtake us as we heal, we know that gratitude moves us toward an emotionally available partner. **I practice gratitude.**

Day 106

Identity

I maintain my own identity in a relationship. If we saw our mothers or other significant women in our lives making their partners the center of their universes, it is hard to know that we deserve to maintain our own separate identity when in a relationship. Fear of getting swallowed by someone who is available, and fear of having their life and passions become ours, can stop us in our tracks. Emotional availability knows that balance is absolutely essential in relationships. Looking around today at successful partnerships, we notice that both partners maintain their own identity. They are not consumed by the relationship. Now, we identify a chameleon-like desire to merge with an individual as a good indication that we are stuck in our issues. At that moment we gently turn our attention inward. We do all the work necessary to discover **ourselves**. We are not our mothers. We do not have to repeat any behavior that we feel is less than healthy. Instead we maintain our own lives. **Today I maintain and nurture my own separate identity when in relationship with a partner.**

Day 107

My Body

I love my body. Women often have very complicated relationships with our bodies. We are bombarded every day with images of the "ideal" feminine body—a body type that is unrealistic for all but 10% of the female population. The female body around potential partners becomes even more problematic when we date. We are taught that we must have a good body to attract a partner; however, healing is about honoring our whole self. Freedom means that we no longer objectify ourselves. Now we know that our bodies are a miracle. Women's bodies experience pleasure no matter what our relationship status, our body size, or our age. To heal, we now explore all the ways that our body supports us. We thank our body for all it does for us every day. Today let's exalt our bodies by treating ourselves to various pleasures such as a nice walk in the fresh air, a warm bubble bath with lit candles, a massage, a hug, a cup of tea, or nurturing foods. **I know my body is not a vehicle to attract a partner. I love and honor my body.**

Day 108

Saying No

I am able to say "no" with my voice. Many of us don't understand that

'No' is a complete sentence. We often mute our own voices, apologize for our needs, and do not feel safe in setting boundaries. However, we say through our behavior what we cannot say with our voices. For example, if we are too afraid of relationships then we run from emotionally available people or we choose unavailable individuals where there is no chance for real intimacy. Saying "no" when we want to say "no" is the antidote to the race from intimacy. Sometimes we may be tempted to add a long explanation when we say "no," but saying "no" is enough. It is a skill we need to develop. Speaking our truth and getting more comfortable saying "no" helps us to choose available people. Saying "no" helps us establish the limits of where we begin and end, what we want in our lives, and what we don't. When we use our voices, we hear with new clarity ourselves saying "no"—and saying "yes." **I don't have to add a long explanation when I say "no" today. I know that I can say "yes" to an emotionally available partner.**

Day 109

Limits and Boundaries

I set limits and boundaries with potential partners. A boundary defines where we begin and end, and where our partner begins and ends. When we set boundaries with someone, we make it easier for them to act appropriately with us. Boundaries help them and us. Today especially, when women and men are confused about what is appropriate and what the other person wants, it is tremendously appropriate to set the boundaries that keep us comfortable in a partnership. If we need to see a person three times a week, we say that. If we cannot accept personal calls at work, we let an individual know. If we need space, we are up front. We make our boundaries count by not expecting another person to maintain our boundaries for us. The boundaries **we** set are ultimately **our** responsibility. We set limits, maintain parameters, or re-negotiate boundaries as necessary. People can take it when we set limits because boundary setting is a gift that lets another person know what does and does not work for us. **I set boundaries with a potential partner.**

Day 110

Belief

I believe in myself. Resolving our partnership issues isn't always fun or painless. Our dedication to this process is amazing. It gives credence to our commitment to our own selves. We have done well in life so far. We have seen ourselves move through many events. It feels good to know we have faith in ourselves, to thank ourselves for our work, and to honor all the ways we are showing up for ourselves. Today let's review our time in this healing process by listing all the good reasons we have to believe in ourselves and all of our estimable acts. If we find ourselves getting down on ourselves or on our process from time to time, we can take out this list as a reminder of how much we have done to heal our partnership issues. This list is a reminder of how strongly we believe in ourselves. **I am someone to be believed in.**

Day 111

Sincerity

I place my thoughts and feelings on the table. It feels good to be sincere; however, many of us have come to believe that sincerity is impossible in an intimate relationship. Because we have gravitated toward unavailable people, we have had experiences with others who were unable to respond to our honesty. Many of us now fear that frankness will drive another person away; yet speaking with sincerity actually gives us a chance to hear ourselves say something out loud. Honesty also offers the other person the chance to know us, which is a divine gift. Our needs, thoughts, and feelings are important. We deserve to be seen and heard. For the next twenty-four hours we make a courageous decision to tell the truth. **Today I speak my truth so that my partner can hear me.**

Day 112

Objectivity

I see others objectively. Here's a shocking and dispassionate idea: let's look at a potential partner as we would a science experiment. Because all our programming about partnership has caused us so much pain in the past, we have most often been unable to see the truth about a person. We are used to seeing what we want to see in others. Healing is about being objective, though. Healing means that we actually see the individual in front of us. We notice them. With practice we become better and better at not transferring all our prejudices onto a potential partner. Letting go of our egos and our subjectivity takes practice and courage. We must release all of our old conceptions of people. To see each individual as a science experiment we need to ask questions. Some sample questions are: "What qualities do we detect? What do we observe in this person? How are we responding to them?" Today we know that seeing details and behaviors of potential partners transfers information that is necessary for making good decisions about them. Now we look clearly at the individual in front of us. **Today I release all my subjective ideas about a person. I see them clearly.**

Day 113

Energy Boundaries

I keep my energy boundaries for fun. Our energy is our own; we only have to share it with another person if we choose. Some people do not believe in energy, yet most of us have heard the term "energy vampire." If someone seems to be trying desperately to get our attention or is speaking to us without love, we can use an energetic shield to protect ourselves. The practice of constructing energy boundaries keeps out all negativity. It also can promote positive feelings. One technique is to imagine ourselves covered by a bell-shaped, translucent coating that is permeable only by joy and light. As the bell touches the ground, we pull up a loving golden light to surround us while minerals and animals of the earth go ping-ponging around the coating of our bell to deflect any negative energy that protrudes into our safe energetic space. Whether we use a technique such as the bell shape, or simply cross our ankles and touch our thumbs to one another, we can contain our energy. These techniques might not be for everyone; however, they do work. **Today I use energetic techniques to keep myself safe.**

Day 114

Privacy

I keep my privacy in a relationship. Ultimately we can't say the wrong thing to the right person; however, we do have the ability to maintain our privacy. The individual in our lives does not need to know all about us or all about our partnership history. We do not want to overwhelm a potential partner by telling them too much. If we want to share something, we are always welcome to. We also give ourselves permission to maintain our privacy. If information does not pertain to health issues or is not dangerous in any way if left unsaid, we are always entitled to share only what we want. We don't have to tell a potential partner something that might turn them off. We deserve a wonderful person. Now we say what feels right to them. **Today I abstain from overwhelming a person.**

Day 115

Boundaries

I know my boundaries and I hold them. Because we been in unfulfilling relationships for so long, we may not know that maintaining our boundaries with another person is our responsibility. A boundary is a limit that makes us comfortable. Once we set a boundary with a person, it is important to note that **we** set the limit. We can continually check in with ourselves and determine if we want to re-negotiate our boundary; however, we can never expect another person to uphold our boundary if we don't or can't. To have a fulfilling relationship, we need to think a boundary through. If we believe it is a boundary we want to uphold and that can be upheld within the context of our partnership, we make a decision to protect our own boundaries. Even if the challenge is great, we can do it. **Our** boundary is ultimately not the responsibility of another. Today we release built-in resentments at other people by knowing our boundaries and by sustaining them. **Today I define, maintain, or re-negotiate my own boundaries.**

Day 116

Inner Child

I keep my inner child safe. If no one cared about us being in a relationship when we were children because they were too self-involved or if they cared **only** about our being partnered, our inner child may still have significant partnership programming. It follows then that our inner child either doesn't care about us being partnering, or cares way too much. Now whenever we are in an emotionally charged relationship situation, it's important to be the adult and keep our inner child safe. Though this practice might not be for everyone, one option is to leave our inner child at the park or playground so that she does not have to go through a frightening experience. (This always works as long as we do not forget to pick her up afterwards!) Talking to our inner child with love always work miracles as well. Today we shelter our inner child. We know that once that tender part of us is taken care of, the emotionally mature adult in us can emerge. **For difficult situations, I leave my inner child where she can play and then remember to return for her.**

Day 117

Self-Trust

I love to trust myself. Relying on ourselves to practice self-love on this journey builds self-trust. In fact, love without trust is impossible. Day by bay, loving interaction by loving interaction, we begin to have a love affair with the one who deserves our love the most—ourselves. We build trust one day at a time. Trust means that we protect ourselves, give ourselves the best of everything, and accept every part of ourselves. We even accept the parts that make us uncomfortable. Trust is confidence in our integrity, strength, and skill. Today we know that we are trustworthy and trusted. We deserve a wonderful, available person. **I am trustworthy.**

Day 118

Journaling

I keep a record of my progress in relationships. Keeping a journal is a wonderful aid to our healing. Positive experiences happen as we walk this path. Even if we only write about how afraid we are that we will never heal our partnership issues, the act of keeping a record enables us to concretely process our journey. One suggestion is to write three things we are grateful for, three things we did well, and three things we could do better each day. By journaling, we chart our upward movement, get useful insights on our interactions with potential partners, and celebrate our successes. Today we record our hopes, challenges, and successes as we move toward a relationship with an emotionally available partner. **I keep my journal up to date because it keeps me informed.**

Day 119

Frankness

I am direct. Directness solves many complications. It is the simple solution to a complex problem. Women in our culture are not often taught to directly express our needs and feelings; however, frankness is a skill those of us healing our fears of partnership need to learn. Being stuck is about knowing how we feel, yet being too intimidated to tell another person. Now that we are healing, we take the risk to put frankness into practice on a daily basis. We know that directness solves many problems. The responses we get to our honest sharing range from mild surprise to gratitude when we tell the truth. Whatever the reaction, though, we continue to practice being honest. It gives our world a bit of what it needs—the truth. **Today I tell the truth.**

Day 120

Meditation

I love to practice meditation.

"Prayer is talking to our Higher Power. Meditating is listening to our Higher Power's answers."—Anonymous

Meditation is a practice that gives us the chance to see what's going on. We quiet the mind and connect to the universe. While sitting still can be hard for us at first, soon it begins to feel good. When we meditate, we find that our lives start to flow more smoothly. Important ideas pop into our consciousness when we rest our minds. We get insight because we are being brought back to the present moment. Often, if we have a question, letting the energy of the universe in by getting still and silent helps unravel our next step. How do we do it, though? Learning to meditate can be done from a book, a teacher, or from a good friend who knows how to practice. Then once we learn how to meditate, meditation can be practiced in many ways. We can practice meditation alone, with a group, with our partner, sitting in the lotus position, lying on the bed listening to soft music, or by some other method. Whatever way we practice meditating, the experience gets us closer to ourselves. Meditation teaches us how to love more effectively. Today we use the tool of meditation to be present. **I take some quiet time to meditate.**

Chapter Summary: Building confidence takes work. As you finish this chapter, you may find you are already using these techniques or you may realize that many of the skills outlined in this chapter are not currently in your repertoire. No matter where you are, the steady practice of these tools helps you heal your partnership issues.

Right now, take a few minutes to identify 3 tools from this chapter that you would like to try. Look at your schedule and determine when you could implement these magical ideas. Make note of at least 1 tool that you used in the past week. Finally, make a decision to pat yourself on the back every time you find yourself using one of these strategies. You are worth the effort!

You have done the work of incorporating these confidence-building exercises in your daily life to make you stronger as you move into the next phase. Then as you start to interact with potential partners, you rely on these practices to sustain you.

Phase I Summary: Now that you have reached the end of **Phase I**, congratulate yourself on a job well done! You have a much greater understanding of yourself at this time. You see the reasons you chose unavailable people, you have compassion for yourself when you notice your old behavior popping up, you love yourself more completely, and you have a body of tools to help you maintain your strength. At this point you may notice that you are feeling stronger. This is the result of all your hard work! Now you can move on with courage to **Phase II**—Understanding Other People.

Right now you may be chomping at the bit to get out there in the dating pool, you may have fears surfacing about interacting with potential partners, or you may have already begun dating. Wherever you are, you are in exactly the right place. Trust yourself. The next chapters will guide you through the process of meeting other people with awareness. Just remember to enjoy yourself as you enter **Phase II**.

Phase II

♥♥♥♥

Understanding

Other People

·5·

Dating Is a Great

Opportunity!

In this chapter, you will learn how to support yourself as you interact with potential partners. You will discover new ways to meet people, how to see individuals instead of stereotypes, and why dating gives you a chance to get to know yourself better. Dating is challenging for everyone, but it can be very rewarding. Take a deep breath and relax. Each day that you interact with potential partners, you are getting closer to the person who can fulfill you.

Day 121

Dating

I see dating as a great opportunity to explore my responses to potential partners. Dating can be painful. It sometimes seems like as we date we are either being rejected or having to reject someone else. Even though it is tough, dating is a great opportunity. When we date we get to explore our responses to people. We do need the experience, but where do we go to meet others? Online dating services, sporting events, social clubs, matchmakers, asking friends to set us up, and interesting classes all offer opportunities to meet single, available individuals who want to meet women just like us. A double or even triple date is also a great, low-pressure dating idea in which each person has a chance to meet several single people while feeling comfortable around her/his friends at the same time. Whatever dating options we choose to explore, let's remember that dating is challenging for everybody. In fact, talking about the nervousness and the experience is a great way to connect with someone, understand more about them, and evaluate their responses to life. **Today I know that I am not on a date alone as I explore my interactions with a potential partner.**

Day 122

Dating Several Potential Partners at a Time

I notice my responses when I date several people at a time. Dating several people at a time offers us a great opportunity to compare our responses to individuals. Do we want to get the attention of the person who is more unavailable? Do we hold on to our original attraction even if it has faded? Are we more afraid of a person who is available? Do we compare people's physical characteristics? Do we favor the appearance of the charmers more? Dating several potential partners at a time is a chance to get closer to ourselves. It is a great opportunity to see our partnership issues functioning. Everybody has preferences for dating. For some of us, dating more than one person at a time is challenging. We may decide we cannot handle all the information. Others of us may feel it is easier to date several people. That way we don't get obsessed with any one person, and don't keep all our eggs in one basket. Whatever way we decide to date is just fine; however, today we know it is appropriate to date several people at a time. **Today I gather information about my patterns if I choose to date several potential partners at one time.**

Day 123

Potential Partners

I see potential partners as peers, friends and companions. Chances are we have had painful interactions with partners in our past. We've made them villains, feared them, or manipulated them. Now, healing our issues leads us to comfort with people. True healing means walking into a room full of potential partners and feeling no fear or compulsion. Healing means no longer having any emotional charge associated with attractive individuals. Obviously, this is a goal on our path. Now we take baby-steps to reach this type of freedom. To start, we re-conceptualize other people. Examining our personal myths about relating, we look at our perceptions of potential partners. Do we see them as users, as dangerous, as passive, as cold? Are we positive they will hurt us? Do we feel we must impress them? Practice interacting with people shows us if our perceptions are true of **all** potential partners. Getting out there gives us the chance to see that most individuals are warm, active, safe, and vulnerable. Mingling teaches us that most individuals are wonderful complements to us in life. Today let's explore the rich wonder of potential partners. We experience freedom when we give ourselves a chance to view people as our peers. **I re-conceptualize partnership.**

Day 124

Kissing

I enjoy kissing if I am so moved.

"Here's to kissing just for the sake of kissing."—Meg Lopez-Cepero

Many of us were never taught that kissing doesn't have to lead to anything else. If we want to, we can conceive of kissing as just a little commitment for the moment. Kissing is not a commitment for more physical intimacy. Kissing does not mean we need to move any farther into physical contact; however, we may if the moment feels right. Through kissing we figure out if we are attracted to a person. Kissing feels good, unless it doesn't. After we kiss a person, we know more clearly if we want to explore further physical contact with them. If we kiss someone and decide we are not interested in learning more about their sexual style, we have risked no more than a small exchange of energy. If we want more information, we move forward. Today we know that we are in charge of our physical progress with a potential partner. **I view kissing as a simple exchange of energy I am to enjoy.**

Day 125

Horn of Plenty

I show myself there is more than enough love and there are more than enough potential life-mates. There are always new love experiences to be had out in the world. People want to connect with us as much as we want to connect with them. We need to remember that many available, loving people are currently waiting for us now. Let's look at all the wonderful ways to meet them. One way to gather our courage to interact with people in the world is to re-conceptualize socializing as a low-pressure activity. Many social clubs exist which are forums for low-pressure interaction. Sports teams, civic minded organizations, and spiritual or religious communities are excellent places to meet people for conversation and activities. Another option is to pursue activities we love, areas we may be waiting to explore until that "someone special" comes into our lives. We don't have to wait. When we take low or no-pressure action to get out into the world, we see the abundance of healthy, warm, loving partners available to us. **I take action to show myself the abundance of potential partners and love on this planet.**

Day 126

Flirtation

I flirt for fun. Flirtation is the re-awakening of our souls to attraction. Flirtation means to act amorously without having serious intentions. This is something many of us don't understand. We certainly know how to flirt. We may even be quite good at it; however, the idea of flirtation is that it is a **trifle**. Flirting is not to be taken seriously. Flirtation is light, fun, and playful. A facet of our partnership issues is taking everything to extremes around potential partners. We may see another person as our salvation, rather than a fun dalliance or someone whose company we very much enjoy. Our focus on the outcome, rather than the magic of attraction and joy, makes us wonder what the person who is flirting with us wants. We may sometimes even deny we are flirting. Flirtations do not have to mean anything, though. Flirtation can be anything from dressing a bit provocatively to batting our eyelashes and briefly touching someone's arm. Flirting can be double entendres or suggestive comments made in conversation. Whatever shape our flirtations take today, we know it is fun to flirt. **I practice flirting without taking it seriously.**

Day 127

Courage

I let a potential partner know how meaningful they are to me. Often women in our society are told to keep a potential partner guessing, to be mysterious and unfathomable. Women who struggle with partnership often take this cultural fiction to the extreme. We are so afraid of others that we refuse to tell them they are important to us. Letting someone know how we feel about them can take enormous strength. If we have had difficult experiences with relationships in the past, believe people only respond to women they have to chase, or have been taught never to let anyone know we care about them, we need all the courage we can muster to tell someone we love them. But courage is fear that has said its prayers. Trust in a Higher Power, prayer, therapy, or support from a friend gives us the ability to let go of our fear as we tell a potential partner the truth. When we are honest and courageous, we walk the path of true love. We move closer to an emotionally available partner. **Today, I surrender my fears and courageously tell a person what they mean to me.**

Day 128

Comfort

I am comfortable with a person who is eager to be with me.

"I don't care to belong to a club that accepts people like me as members."—Groucho Marx

Millions of reasons exist to deflect the love of someone who eagerly pursues us. When we meet an emotionally available individual, we sometimes think negatively. We think, "They must be really hard up to want me." We sometimes distrust a person who wants to be with us. We question their motives and look for the tragic flaw that will expose their undesirability. Many times this is sensible because someone may not really be good for us; however, this is often only our low self-esteem talking. Learning to honor our intuition, while distinguishing it from the voice which tells us we are not good enough, is important. We are magical, lovely, amazing, wonderful women who deserve a happy, content partner who is utterly in love with us. Healing is about developing a comfort level with appropriate, available people who adore us. By doing this work, we are progressing all the time! **Today I know that an emotionally available person who is eager to be with me is sane.**

Day 129

Male and Female Views on Sex

I understand my sexual style.

"Most men think they know a women's whole sexual style after sleeping with her once."—Rose

Men and women have very different ideas about what sexual intimacy means. The difference is biological and emotional. As a rule, men are very connected to their sexual selves. Men also physically express their desire externally. Women on the other hand are more often connected to our heart center. We express sexual desire more subtly. The difference explains why the pairing of men and women is so special; men and women balance each other. When we are in relationships or dating, though, the significance of these differences can become important. Men and women most often categorize sex differently. For instance, many men see sex as a basic need that must be fulfilled. Most women see sex as a beautiful love experience. Neither men nor women are wrong about what sex means to them; however, we women need to protect ourselves. If we want to have sex, that is always OK. The choice to wait is appropriate too. Because health concerns are an issue, as is the tendency of some of us to get emotionally involved once we have sex, today we decide what we want and what will work for us. **I make the choice to be sexual or not based on my desires.**

Day 130

Adult Love

I let myself love the way a normal adult woman loves. No matter our age, many of us revert to the lover we were when we first began to interact with partners. We may feel as awkward as a teenager as we date. Our relational challenges have literally stunted our emotional growth. This can be very frustrating as we heal. Today if we feel like an adolescent around potential partners, it is essential to begin to love as an adult woman loves. Visualizing what a lover our age looks like, how she responds to a person, and what she enjoys in connecting with a partner gives us the chance to act our age in relationships. By "acting as if" we were that woman; we utilize our often highly developed skills at playacting for **our** benefit. The adult lover in us is compassionate, knowledgeable, free, available, kind, and warm. She is waiting for us to liberate her. She does not play games; instead, she truly cherishes the person in her life. **I "act as if" I am an emotionally adult woman.**

Day 131

Spring Fever

I embrace spring fever. Spring is the time of year when new growth starts in the ground. Things are starting to get shaken up. The winds begin to blow sweetly. Attractions start to heat up between partners. Love is in the air as the weather becomes warmer, as green shoots grow, and as flowers begin to bloom. As the energy of growth, warmth, and love starts to take root, we often feel spring fever. No matter what our partnerships status, this springtime let's flirt. If we are in a partnership, we can enjoy the sensations of springtime. We can refocus our love, attention, and care on our partner. Spring is the time to strew the bed with flowers. It offers us a chance to play outside with our love in the warm weather. If we are single, spring is a great time to get outside and connect with potential partners. We enjoy watching them. We admire their vitality. As we stand in awe of the joys of desire, we know this is the season to play. **For this day I let springtime into my heart.**

Day 132

Beauty

I see the beauty in men. Men are amazing creatures with much love to give, the ability to change and grow, and a true ability to appreciate the feminine. Male beauty comes in many forms: physical, spiritual, and emotional. The physical form of male beauty has been immortalized for centuries. The spiritual beauty of men also shines. It illuminates the male ability to give, to listen, to change, and to grow. Many brave men are exploring their emotions today. Men are figuring themselves out using literature that exists for the emotionally unavailable man, process groups, and interactions with women. Every interaction with men that **we** undertake on the journey to heal our partnership issues gives us the chance to observe the emotional beauty of men. When we hear men share about many of the same emotions we feel, it is comforting to get closer to that vulnerable, softer part of men. Because men are so amazing, we honor them for their beauty—body, mind, and spirit. **Today I honor men for all the beauty they possess.**

Day 133

Practicalities

I consider practicalities as I interact with potential partners. On our journey to heal our partnership issues, there are many practicalities to consider as we interact with people. For our own protection, we take precautions when meeting potential partners. We may want to set boundaries for ourselves on a date. We could choose to meet with a person in a public place the first few times we see them or estimate how much time we want to spend with them. Checking in with a trusted friend before and after the date can help. In addition, we could leave ourselves a voicemail message detailing what we think of the individual right after the date. Such painstaking practicalities may not be for everyone, yet these are options for getting a fuller picture of how we experience a potential partner. When we do this, we get information without the immediacy of hormones and feelings. Interacting with people when we have a plan gives us detachment. And when we invest in ourselves, we are present. **Today I get a full picture of a potential partner with the use of effective precautions.**

Day 134

Ambivalence

I deal with my ambivalence. Ambivalence is a placeholder until we decide which direction we want to go. Ambivalence is characterized by a fluctuation between two choices. When we are ambivalent about a person, we experience a simultaneous desire to say or do two different things. Usually we are in the place of ambivalence when we intuitively know which way we want to go, yet do not want to face the facts. For example, if we think a person might be interested in us, sometimes we want to generate a reciprocal interest in them. We want to be attracted to them, but we are uncertain. We move toward them; then we move away. We are only half there. We are not available for the relationship. Ambivalence provides a placeholder until we get clear about where we want to go with an individual. Most of the time when we feel ambivalent about a person, that is giving us information that they may not be right for us or that we aren't comfortable for some reason. Sometimes, though, our ambivalence is motivated by fear. We may feel we are not good enough for someone or we may not feel ready for the responsibility of a relationship. Today we know that ambivalence is telling us something. Now we listen to it with respect. **I let ambivalence teach me about myself.**

Day 135

Looking for Love

I notice if I look for love in places where I won't find an available

partner. There are many wonderful people who fit the type we need. If we continually find potential partners who don't satisfy us, the problem could be that we are looking in the wrong places. If we are frequenting establishments or attending events where we will not find who we need, we now fearlessly look at our behavior. Patronizing events and venues where there is a shortage of available people, or where the attendees do not fit our description of an ideal mate, signals that we need to be aware of our issues. It is helpful to probe ourselves with gentle questions to see if we are going to or staying in places where we could never possibly be satisfied with the patrons. What most of us forget is that we have power to choose where we spend our time. Since our issues often take the guise of dating people we do not connect with in order to avoid getting close and experiencing real intimacy, it takes courage to find someone who is an equal. Today we know that we are worth the effort. **I go where I need to in order to find a person who is available.**

Day 136

Connecting

I embrace connections with people. The great myth of "coupledom" in our culture is that connecting with another is the most important thing in life. It does feel good to couple and to be in a couple; however, being single is good and valid as well. Connection takes courage. We may not be ready to couple at this moment for a variety of reasons. We may not want to. Being a member of a couple is a wonderful place to be, but being single does not prohibit us from connecting with people. There are many relationships we can have with people that will illuminate our healing process. Today we have the option of playing on a team with other people, working on a project with potential partners, enjoying the presence of co-workers at our staff meeting, or connecting with dear friends. Privileging connection with a person on a partnership level can stunt our growth. Today we embrace all connections with people, not just partnerships. **Today I am connected with another.**

Day 137

How an Individual Treats Others

I gather information as I observe a potential partner interacting with other people. A potential partner will generally treat us the same way that they treat other people. Now when we date someone, we notice how they treat their friends, our friends, or colleagues of ours. It is common knowledge that a person's behavior toward service workers is important; noticing how an individual interacts with other people is also significant. Whenever we see our partner interact with our peers, we pay special attention. Do they share appropriately with them? Are they attentive, respectful, courteous, and honest whether the people are co-workers, friends, "ex"-partners, older or younger? Do they flirt with or hit on others? Noticing the interactions of a potential partner around other people provides concrete information which helps us move forward. Then we are free to choose an emotionally available individual. **Today I notice how a person treats other people.**

Day 138

Flirting

I flirt with potential partners I find attractive. There is no harm in flirting. It is fun and good for the soul. Women facing our own partnership issues often put too much emphasis on flirting, though. We sometimes take flirtations very seriously. If an undesirable person flirts with us, we may become convinced that they want a relationship. Then we run away from them. If a desirable person flirts with us, we may think that they want a relationship with us. Then we are disappointed when no partnership materializes. Many results can occur if we have taken flirting too seriously in any way. Today we may be out of practice in flirting, we may believe we can't do it, or we may find it too frightening. Flirting feels good, though. It is a free, harmless, enjoyable pleasure. Today is the time to flex our flirting muscles, if we want to. **I flirt for fun when I am attracted to a potential partner.**

Day 139

Investing in Potential Partners

I know how to have an abundance of people in my life without getting hooked in. In the past, whenever a person wasn't available, we may have labeled them, thrown out their number, or "blackballed" them. Discerning the unavailable person from someone who is ready to make a commitment to us is necessary; however, as we progress we may want to hold people in our lives. Even if they are not "The One," they may be great company. Human beings are wonderful to know. Humans are fun, playful, active, interesting, and creative. Keeping people as friends is a highly developed skill. We must let go of the fantasy of that person suddenly becoming available to us for more than friendship. Having an abundance of people in our lives is pleasurable if we can avoid getting wrapped up in them. No matter where we are in our process, we now know that the principle of investing in others is a possibility. Today if we choose to keep someone in our lives, we can build our network. **Today I am capable of keeping an individual who is unavailable for partnership as my friend if I am comfortable with that.**

Day 140

Equality

I treat potential partners as I want to be treated. While stuck in our partnership issues, we may have treated other people shockingly. Conversely, we may have viewed them with total awe. Common treatment of people resulting from our emotional shakiness has been ignoring, yelling, sulking, pouting, blaming, nagging, holding them to unreasonable expectations, throwing things, or abruptly leaving a relationship. Today these behaviors are no longer useful for us. We firmly reject them. Our partners deserve good treatment. Whatever our histories of treating other people, we know that today is the time to begin again. Now we treat our partners lovingly. This does not mean that we accept behavior from another person that is less than nurturing. If we need to take care of ourselves with an individual, we do that swiftly and effectively; however, we act with fairness and compassion wherever possible. Now we know that love, tolerance, honesty, communication, and forgiveness are appropriate ways to interact with people. For today we let go of all behaviors that no longer serve us as we heal our partnership issues. **I practice new behaviors with the person in my life.**

Day 141

Timing

I have impeccable timing in communicating with a partner. Timing is important. If a person is distracted, playing video games, seems to be mulling over a problem, or is concerned about work or the economy, chances are that is not the best time to approach them with heavy issues. Women are generally good at understanding timing; however, many of us have had challenging experiences trying to communicate with our partners. Often we have let something go for too long. Then we have exploded at someone or have refused to communicate at all with a person for lack of skill. Whatever our experience, understanding people's patterns is essential to effective communication. If we do not have the skill set we would like in terms of understanding timing, there is a wealth of information on effective communication. (Some good resources are listed at the back of this book.) When we *want what we want when we want it*, it may not be the best time to connect with our partner. Usually a good rule of thumb is to wait at least five minutes before we discuss an important issue with a person. Now we know that the needs of the partner in our life deserve to be respected just as do our own needs. Today we judge timing correctly, and we know we deserve to be heard when it is appropriate. **I communicate when the time is right.**

Day 142

Agendas

I let go of my agendas. Our agendas can keep us stuck. Agendas are problematic. If we are completely committed to the plans we have set for our interaction or mode of relating to a person, we have an inability to be present and flowing with the process of life. Disappointment may follow. When many of us are disappointed, the person then can become our target rather than a real human being. We forget that they have their own needs and feelings. Today we stop the cycle. If we notice that we have an agenda for any situation or relationship, we are aware of it. We examine the plans we have without judgment. Then we accept where we are now, check in to see how we are feeling behind the agenda, and let go of the agenda. If we feel that a person has a plan for us, we do not step into the role assigned for us or retaliate with an outline of our own. We question them about their intentions or we excuse ourselves. Now we know that agendas do not help a relationship. We know that agendas keep us trapped. **Today I release all hidden agendas.**

Day 143

Acceptance

I accept other's limitations. Acceptance does not mean approval. Though we may not like someone's behavior, the person is still a miraculous creation. They are precious. If someone is limited in their ability to give us what we need, we use that information wisely. We release them without labeling. Healing is not about judging another for what they can or cannot do in relationships. It is about loving ourselves enough to let go of a person if it is clear that they cannot show up for us. The other option is to accept their inabilities if there are other pay-offs from being with them. **Today I know what I need. I accept other's limitations.**

<h2 style="text-align:center">Day 144</h2>

Running Away

I let myself interact with a person without running away from them.

"Give a person three chances to know you."—Lydia Yinger

Giving appropriate people three chances to know us takes guts. When we do this we get a chance to see them seeing us. Obviously giving an individual three chances is not a hard and fast rule. One date may be more than enough to tell if we do not want to see a person again. The problem is that for many of us it takes discipline to actually let a person get to know us. We may want to run away from them, especially if they seem "boring." Because drama translates to excitement for many of us, we are uncomfortable with a person who is truly available. There is no "hook." It may take practice for some of us to let ourselves experience how an individual feels to us without getting rid of them. Now as we date someone, we gather more information to decide if they are a good choice for our continued sharing. With practice, patience, and time, our interactions with potential partners move us into healthy relationships. **For this day only, I decide to let a person get to know me without running away from them.**

<h2 style="text-align:center">Day 145</h2>

Who I Want

I am clear about who I want. Attraction is one part of the equation in relationships; knowing what behaviors and qualities in a person are desirable for us is another. Doing the research of interacting with potential partners, while keeping an awareness of ourselves, teaches us who **we** want. It is essential to gaining perspective. However, interaction with self-awareness can seem extremely intimidating to many of us. We have usually tuned in to what someone else wanted. A different challenge we may have faced was being so overwhelmed by an attractive individual that we lost ourselves. The only way to achieve clarity about ourselves is to interact with people, though. We each deserve a wonderful partner who is good for us; and they are out there waiting. Today we get the support we need when interacting with potential partners. **I clearly know what I need in a partner today.**

Day 146

Categories

I abstain from categorizing people. Thinking outside the box characterizes emotional availability. Making categories is a function of our ego. Our ego wants clear definitions in order to feel safe. We believe that if we know where people fit in categories, then we can position ourselves to experience the least amount of hurt. For example, if we believe people are "out of our league," then we forget to see that there is a human being inside of them. Once they were little and dreamed of being their favorite cartoon character. They liked to eat sugar cereal. They have dreams and desires now. Similarly, if we think a person is "below" us, we miss their wonderful sensitivity, strength, and humor. Emotional availability knows that this person in front of us is not just a prop. They are a real person with dreams, feelings, needs, insecurities, and passions. As we heal our partnership issues, we don't want to diminish love experiences, other people, or our partnerships. Today we avoid shoving people into categories. **I let go of all the categories I have used to box other people in.**

Day 147

Mind Reading

I abstain from all mind reading. Mind reading can get us into trouble. When we think we know what a person is thinking or feeling, we may be incorrect. The only way to know for sure what someone else is thinking is to risk involvement. We have to ask questions. The reason many of us detour into mind reading is that in our own heads we are in control (or so we think.) In our minds we develop elaborate explanations for a person's behavior. We are often quite sure we are correct. Although mind reading may seem less dangerous than actually getting the information we need, mind reading blocks love from radiating throughout our partnership. Chances are we are dead wrong in our assumptions anyway. Now we know that our tendency to mind read can strangle the love of even the best partnership. It is not about relating, it is about **our** mind. It is about control. Today we fearlessly let go of all mind reading behavior. **I check things out with my partner when I feel tempted to read their mind.**

Day 148

Getting Out There

Today I get out in the world. Many people are waiting to meet women just like us. People want to meet us as much as we love to meet them. Figuring out what type of person we want helps us as we get out in the world to mingle. Then to meet potential partners, we must figure out areas to meet a potential life-mate. A starter list of venues to meet people include job fairs, hiking clubs, fishing trips, national parks, canoeing activities, civic organizations, singles events, parties, set ups, ice skating rinks, personal ads, financial seminars, the elevator at work, the racetrack, the county fair, dance clubs, the yacht club, classes, workshops, neighborhood meetings, volunteer opportunities, and church or temple. Partners are available and seeking wonderful women. If we pursue an activity we enjoy, chances are we will meet someone who has similar interests and wants a woman just like us. **Today I mingle in select areas.**

Day 149

Judgments

I avoid judgments and I see individuals. Our whole society is about judgments. It can be extremely challenging for us to emerge from all the propaganda we have been taught about partnership. Many of us are taught that potential partners are all only after sex, want younger women, are emotional cripples, or are scary. These judgments completely negate the individual person standing in front of us, though. We forget that they have feelings and desires when we judge them. We forget that they have a favorite movie, a favorite breakfast food, a favorite childhood picture book. The next time we find ourselves making a judgment about our partner or any person, we stop ourselves. We realize that we need to truly see **them**. Our judgments put pressure on **us**; judgments do not allow us to truly cherish others. Today we realize that releasing judgments doesn't mean we can't have opinions; however, whenever we are tempted to judge, we remember that there is a human spirit inside of our partner. **Today I see the person in front of me without judgments.**

Day 150

Safety

I let safe people in. Many women in our culture have been told to be kind to everyone, to put other people's needs first, and to be polite at all costs. Now we see the huge burden we have placed on ourselves, and others, by ignoring our own needs for safety. Using all our tools today of intuition, life experiences, and a connection with a Higher Power, we trust our own wisdom to know who is safe to let into our lives. Sitting quietly with ourselves, we tune into the part of us that can judge who is a safe partner, and who is not. We may not be perfect in honoring ourselves right away, the process may take time, and we may make poor judgment calls, yet our choices do improve. Safe people are waiting for us to let them in. Now when we decide that someone is appropriate to let into our world, we gently open our heart. **For this day only, I choose safe people to let in.**

Day 151

Ignoring People

I abstain from ignoring potential partners. Often we have been overlooked in the past by our partners, our parents, or significant people in our lives. Now we just continue the cycle. The problem is that people who have been disregarded have deep doubts about their worth. In order to stop passing on what we know, it is imperative to stop slighting people. Sometimes we neglect others because we can't handle our feelings, because we feel responsible for everyone else's needs and can't take care of our own, or because we need to feel superior to other people. Whatever the reason, whenever we ignore others, we perpetuate a damaging cycle. Our partners deserve to be noticed. While making a decision to pay appropriate attention to people takes practice, we can do it one day at a time. **I pay attention to my partner.**

Chapter Summary: Dating **is** a great opportunity. You are getting to know yourself better all the time. By now, you are interacting with potential partners and getting lots of information. You are taking care of yourself in powerful ways. You are finally getting a chance to date as an adult. You are also starting to see the truth about other people. At this point in your process, you may notice a huge shift in the way you interact with others. You may feel attracted to those you would never have considered before. This is normal! You are exactly where you are supposed to be.

Today, reflect on 4 ways that you are taking care of yourself differently on dates. Write down 3 venues to meet people that you would like to try out in the future. Notice 2 ways you are starting to see potential partners in a different light. Most importantly, give yourself a hand for getting out there in the first place!

Dating can be challenging and painful; your commitment is tremendous. If things seem bleak when you interact with others, this is to be expected. Just keep on going. You are getting better all the time. Remember that the process of getting out in the world to date is imperative to healing your partnership issues. As you get practice in the dating world, you are positioning yourself to meet available people who can meet your needs.

Now you may be asking several questions. How do you know when a person is available? How do you identify signs of emotional unavailability at work in others? What do you do if you determine that a person can't meet your needs? The next chapter gives you the answers you need to identify and deal with the emotionally unavailable type.

·6·

Emotionally Available

or Not?

This chapter you will help you determine an individual's availability quotient. You will learn to maintain realistic expectations of yourself and of your partner, how to identify signs of emotional unavailability in potential partners, and how to let an emotionally available person into your heart. Enjoy this part of the process. It will make you stronger.

Day 152

The Emotionally Available Partner

I seek an available partner. Our culture teaches us that we should seek out someone where the attraction is magnetic; often these people are dangerous, though. They may be critical, married, or emotionally unavailable in some other way. Almost always there is a snafu involved in a relationship with an emotionally unavailable person. Things rarely go smoothly. Most of us can clearly identify the unavailable person in our lives. Now, in order to heal, we seek an emotionally available partner. As we interact with people and meet an available person, we initially perceive a difference. We feel happier. There is a healthy exchange of energy in the partnership. Life progresses lightly and calmly. Having an available partner in our lives doesn't ensure a problem-free relationship; however, an emotionally rich partnership enhances our lives. **Today I seek an available person and I choose an available partner.**

Day 153

Unavailable

I let go of all unavailable people. People who say one thing but do another, send mixed messages, and confuse us are people who are unavailable. Emotionally unavailable people: make dates then breaking them, are married or in a long term relationship, are alcoholics or compulsive gamblers, angry, physically abusive, or imprisoned, don't want to be in a relationship with us, are misogynistic, passive-aggressive, or frequently late, are still connected to their "ex," don't initiate, put no energy out, keep us guessing, flirt with other people, are not attracted to us, control us, judge us, are hesitant in some way, or are inconsistent. Unavailable people are challenging to be with. If we find ourselves attracted to them and getting caught up in the drama, it may be time for us to examine our own behaviors. Are we also unavailable? Do we make it easy for people to act this way with us? Do we make them upset or prone to react? Being the partner we seek is always the answer to being emotionally available. If we are unavailable, we notice. Whether we must generate more clarity in ourselves up front about what we need in and expect in a partner, if we must set more boundaries along the way with an unavailable person, or if we must just let an individual go, today we say goodbye to the unavailable type. **Today, I release all need for unavailable people in my life.**

Day 154

Facing Reality

I face reality. Facing reality is sometimes not pleasant but it can save us future trouble. If a person does not want to commit to us or is emotionally shut down, chances are they are not emotionally available. The sooner we face reality about where they are and what they can do in a relationship with us, the sooner we are free to choose someone who gives us what we need. If we can't let an unavailable person go, though, that is always OK; however, we then need to face reality about **ourselves**. Chances are if we are attracted to an emotionally distant individual, then we are stuck in our fears of commitment too. We do not judge others or ourselves if this is the case. We only acknowledge the information. Everything we do is fine. *It is always OK to be with whoever we need to be with, whenever we need to be with them.* If we are not getting the true satisfaction we need from someone, however, we face the facts today. **I face the facts about a potential partner.**

Day 155

Seeing

I see when people are unavailable and incapable. When we are stuck in our fears of partnership, we pretend that an individual is available. We are unwilling to see the facts about an unavailable potential partner. We deny the truth. We often are so good at denial that we deceive ourselves. Denial is just a symptom of our issues, though. It's hard and it hurts when people can't give us what we want; however, lying to ourselves ultimately causes us more pain than the pain we are running from. It gets us into long relationships that go nowhere. Today we have the alternative of fearlessly facing the truth about a person. If an individual is unavailable and incapable, we face the facts. Now we use the information we gather about a person without judging, blaming, or criticizing them. We face the truth with compassion for the other person. Then we let go of them if we need to. **For the next 24 hours I take the blinders off!**

Day 156

Understanding

I understand the situation.

"Give it the friend test. Would it bother me if my friend did it?"—Meg Lopez-Cepero

When we are stuck, it is hard to see the truth. Getting quiet, centered, and getting help to understand an uncomfortable relationship situation is essential. For example, one woman was very hurt that her fiancé spent so much time with his family before their wedding. Her partnership issues had trapped her in selfishness and self-centeredness. She had set other people up as the enemy. Often we, too, cannot see a relationship with any perspective when we are so blinded by our own perceptions. Whether we make more of a comment, gesture or perceived slight than it warrants, or whether we go to the other extreme and deny the impact of a person's behavior on our serenity, understanding is imperative. Friends, writing, meditation, therapy, and reflection are all tools to help us attain clarity about a situation with our partner. To heal her challenge, the woman in the example above talked to several good friends to understand the situation. She realized his actions were not about her. Then she was able to give her fiancé his freedom without taking things personally. Now they are happily married. We all require a reality check like this from time to time. The good news is that now we know how to get the support we need. **For this day only, I gain perspective on my relationship.**

Day 157

The Unavailable Man

I release all unavailable men. There are many books describing emotional unavailability on the male level. Any man who is currently in a relationship, married, experiencing serious emotional problems, abusive, neglectful, sending mixed messages, commitment phobic, ambivalent about us, an active alcoholic or drug abuser, a workaholic, or a compulsive gambler is unavailable. It is always OK for us to choose a man who cannot give us what we need; however, learning to recognize danger signals early in a relationship helps us in the long run. Facing reality about a man's unavailability can mean pain for us in the moment, yet by releasing such a man we are opening ourselves to the possibility of meeting someone available. All of us deserve an emotionally available partner. When we let go of the unavailable type, we open the door to someone wonderful. **Today if I notice that a man is unavailable, I know I can make the decision to let go of him.**

Day 158

Entanglement

I disentangle myself from my pattern of running from available people. We usually have many old ideas about partnership. Our interactions with unavailable people have confirmed what we fear is true about potential partners in general: that they are dangerous, frightening, unfriendly, and/or cold. A fear of people characterizes our partnership issues. Being with an unavailable partner has hurt us, yet the reason we have many times chosen to be with someone who can't or won't commit to us is because it is familiar. Now as we interact with potential partners and meet available people, we find individuals who represent the very opposite of our fears. The problem is that whenever we do find people who are safe and comforting, we most often don't know how to respond. These available people often send us running! If this happens to us, we do not need to fear. The universe is bringing us a wonderful, available partner right now. All we need to do is focus on the process and love ourselves. Healing means disentangling from our dysfunctional pattern. Healing is a process of opening ourselves up to someone who gives us what we need—an emotionally available person. **I release unavailable people and choose someone nurturing and open.**

Day 159

Practicalities

I know which people to avoid. Ultimately our rebellion and willfulness has contributed to our challenges in past relationships. No one has ever been able to tell us who to be with. We have simply never been willing or able to listen to "authorities" on the subject. Today, we avoid this problem by becoming our own authority. We decide for ourselves what types of people to side-step. Knowing we deserve available people, and having boundaries about what types of individuals work for us, is essential. While this sounds harsh, today we generate a list of people who most probably are not candidates for healthy relationships. To get the ball rolling we now avoid: married people, financially unstable individuals, active drug addicts and alcoholics, people with serious emotional problems, and those who yell or have abusive pasts. Certainly there are exceptions, yet we deserve available people in our lives. There are plenty of stable, adorable, loving potential partners who want women just like us. It is always OK to be with who we want, whenever we want to be with them. The only important qualification is that we examine how this person makes us feel and truly listen to **our** own feelings. **Today I create a list of people who I consider unavailable, and then I choose an available partner.**

Day 160

Red Flags

I pay attention to all red flags. If a person looks good and fits many of the characteristics of our ideal mate, sometimes we don't want to see the red flags. We are tempted to ignore the signals that something is not adding up. When someone tells us information, and that is usually within the first hour of knowing them, we need to hear them. Even if this information goes counter to our idealized perceptions of what they **could** be, we need to honor the facts. We think, "They could be 'The One!'" Healing means that we women trust **all** our senses. Now we stay alert to the red flags a person may display at the beginning of a relationship. If a person is still discussing their "ex," is angry, or is inconsiderate, it is important for us to notice. We must really take this information to heart. It may be disappointing in the moment to notice red flags; however, we save ourselves a lot of pain in the long run. No one will be perfect, but the beginning of a relationship is when we are all on our best behavior. Now we know that initial red flags deserve our attention. **I notice and respect any red flags a potential partner displays.**

Day 161

Leading Questions

I do not take the bait when asked a leading question if I do not want to. When someone asks us a leading question, it is a red flag. A leading question is meant to open a can of worms, it expects a certain answer, and it is provocative. Although asking a leading question doesn't make someone bad, it does signify that they are not letting things flow. They may have a hidden agenda. Questions about sex, our incomes, and even our habits, can be uncomfortable if posed too soon in a relationship. Typically we have answered questions we felt uncomfortable with in order to appease or keep a partner. Our fear that we might offend someone has often taken precedence over acknowledging what we find invasive. Today we know that we do not need to answer any question a person asks that causes us discomfort. Each time we identify and set boundaries around leading questions with a potential partner, we take a positive step forward. **Today I know that a person who asks leading questions is waving red flags in the air.**

Day 162

Emotionally Available People

I am an emotionally available person. Emotionally available people don't let it ruin their whole day if they have a painful interaction with someone they care about, obsess on someone, or behave in less than desirable ways. An emotionally available individual knows that everyone makes mistakes. Emotionally present people know there is always another chance to interact lovingly and to practice new behavior. Emotional availability knows that no one is perfect. It understands that we all experience challenges as we relate. Perfection is an illusion. One painful experience with our partner does not ensure that others will follow. Being emotionally available is letting go of the tape we play that says we always get hurt in relationships. Today we are emotionally available people who know that a wonderful love experience is just around the corner. **I am emotionally available because I know that wonderful love experiences come and go.**

Day 163

Male Disclosure

I honor what men tell me. Men have a gift to give us in dating. Usually in the first hour a man tells us who they are, what their style is in relationships, and what capacity they have for intimacy. The problem is not unwillingness in men to show who they are; the problem is that we are often very good at hearing what we want to hear and seeing what we want to see in potential partners. For example: if a man is still getting over a previous relationship with an "ex" and hasn't completely let go yet, notice. If he says he has a lot of personal problems, listen. This doesn't mean he is not the man for us; however, we need to hear the information. We must determine if a man can meet our needs and what pace will be appropriate to take with him. **Today I listen closely to what a man discloses to me.**

Day 164

Eighty Percent

I decide that 80% is enough.

"No human being is going to be 100% available."—Hillary Flye

Putting our partner's availability on the top of our list is important; however, we need to keep balanced expectations of people. No man or woman will be 100% available. Balance and moderation are essential as we heal our partnership issues. Promoted by the media, our parents and other cultural sources, we believe that the perfect relationship is out there. We think it is just a matter of finding that "someone special." People aren't perfect, though. Perfection is an illusion. That is why our expectations get us in trouble. Giving about 80% to the relationship is acceptable. It leaves the other percentage free for each partner to develop her/his interests. Now we know that giving 80% both within a relationship, and in the world, allows us to be more human. **I have balanced expectations of myself and my partner.**

Day 165

Passive People

I choose to be with a self-actualized person.

"A year before I met him, my husband would have scared me to death."—Jane

Being in an unequal partnership may feel comfortable for us. In the past, it may have felt safer to choose people that we could lead. Then we felt that we had control. Now available, successful, whole people may make us run away in a panic. We feel scared to death that we are not good enough. We are ruled by the fear that we do not deserve a wonderful life-mate. Now we identify that fear as a function of our low self-esteem. To heal, we continue working on ourselves. We know that our comfort level increases as we practice interacting with self-actualized people. Many times we still find ourselves wanting to fix a potential partner; we are almost compelled to. Today, though, we stop ourselves. Then we make a decision to stop taking care of our partner. We let them show up as a mature adult. **I enjoy the company of a rational, adult person.**

Day 166

All Potential Partners

I legalize all people. Today all potential partners are legal for us. Individuals have no charge. They are neither bad nor good. Whatever type of person we want is OK. Spiritual people, married people, construction workers, charmers, financial planners, unavailable people, and kind people are all equal. No one is better or worse. All we have to do is stay in touch with ourselves as we mingle. Now we ask questions to see how we feel in being with this person. Is the charmer narcissistic and exciting, while the kind person is boring but loving? How does this make us feel? Do we get a thrill from flirting with someone with a ring on their finger? What do we want from this person? Can we get what we want from them?

The legalization process seems scary because many of us wish we could just have a rule book to follow; however, the rules are inside of us. Our internal knowing signals who it feels good to be with. Though it is scary, going through the legalization process makes it unnecessary for us to rebel, lose touch with our own signal, attempt to follow rules that dictate who we "should" be with, and run to those who can't possibly be available. Legalization is the part of healing that moves us toward a wonderful person, so today we practice! **Today I know that all people are legal. I explore what type of person I enjoy interacting with.**

My Issues/Their Issues

I make a distinction between my issues and my partner's issues.
Focusing on our own issues and dealing with what is in front of us lets our partner take care of their own life. If a person tries to convince us that we are at the center of their issues, we may become confused and assume that they are correct. For example, one woman was told by her boyfriend of three weeks that he would be on time for their dates if only she didn't nag him. This is not true! She knew that each person is ultimately responsible for their own behavior in relationships. She quickly realized he was not the correct match for her. Then she released him. Now she is happy with a wonderful partner who is on time and knows he's responsible for himself.

If, like her, at any time on our journey we find ourselves getting wrapped up in someone else's issues, we take a time out. Then we do the necessary footwork to gently figure out if that is **our** truth. We are supportive and available when a person asks for help; however, now **we** determine the difference between what our issues are and what belongs to them. **I enjoy separating what belongs to me and what belongs to my partner.**

Day 168

Pigeonholing Others

I keep an open mind whenever I meet a potential partner. "That person seems needy. He's so boring! That one's too macho. They are not successful enough. I want someone more attractive. What a nerd…" Whenever we put an individual in a category like this, it is a good indication that our partnership issues are rearing up. Now we pay attention to the message we are sending ourselves. Seen in this way, judgment is a good opportunity to get closer to ourselves and to our own feelings. Let's remember that whenever we judge another, usually we are judging these same qualities in ourselves. This is not at all necessary. We are all amazing creatures with a purpose on this planet. When we judge, we know only a small amount about this person in front of us. Judgment is based on very little concrete information. In fact, we may later regret our hasty judgments. We can miss out on a wonderful person because of our personal prejudices. We don't appreciate it when others put us "in a box," so now we give others the same respect of not pigeonholing them. The next time we meet a potential partner, we reserve our judgments until we have more information. **I abstain from pigeonholing other people.**

Day 169

Married People

I examine my motives for being involved with a married person. Involvement with a married individual can almost wipe us out. We may be attracted to this kind of unavailability in a person because then there is no real chance of getting close and having to be intimate. Although it will hurt to be with someone who can never really love us the way we want because they already have a partner, that pain actually protects us from having to explore our own blocks to intimacy. When we are involved with married people, it is easy to distract ourselves from our own lives. Everything revolves around that magic moment when they will be ready to love us, when we will get "the cookie," when they will leave their significant other.

There are also many dramatic highs and lows in this type of relationship to divert our attention; however, involvement with a married individual is a difficult and unfulfilling way to live. If we are choosing this path, we look closer at the pain we are causing ourselves. Now we see that it is really our own issues that hook us in. It is always OK to be with a married person if we want; today, however, we ask ourselves gently if that involvement feels good and if this is what we want. **I release a married person if I choose.**

Day 170

Involvement

I am involved in my relationships. Getting involved can seem scary to us. We often have a long history of heartbreaking experiences where involvement with unavailable and/or incapable people caused upset. Real intimacy, however, can only be nurtured through involvement. No person will always be able to meet us, yet as we heal we become better able to ascertain who is available and who isn't. Each day, we learn how to judge situations more skillfully. Today we gain assurance that involvement is safe and worthwhile. Now we choose to be involved with people who are safe. **Today I have the faith in myself to risk involvement with safe people.**

Day 171

Ex-Partners

I see my "ex" clearly. The hook connecting us to one or several of our "ex-partners" can be extremely strong. As we heal, the temptation to return to "ex-partners" can arise. Sometimes we think we have changed so much that we can make it work this time around, we may feel desperate to connect with **any** person (even someone less than nurturing), or we may want to reconnect with someone who will be glad to hear from us. It is always OK to be with any person including our "ex." No matter what course we take, though, it is important to see our "ex" clearly. When we get hooked back into a person from our past, we ask ourselves if they treat us well and if we feel good when we are around them. If our "ex" was very problematic, dangerous, or hurtful, however, we talk to loving friends or support people who remind us of what we need and want in a partner. **I evaluate my response to an "ex-partner" as I would any other potential partner.**

Day 172

Safe People

I trust safe people. The process of healing means trusting safe individuals but safe people may seem boring to many of us. Over and over in the past, we may have chosen partners who were in some way unsafe. We did this because of naiveté, because we were recreating old wounds, or just through bad luck. Now as we heal, the journey to the center of our own issues helps us realize that we deserve to be with people who treat us appropriately. Our challenges around partnership have been hanging on forever just to teach us that we deserve the best. Today we are entitled to dignity in our relationships. Safe people feel good to be around. No one will ever be 100% safe and appropriate because we all have our issues; however, safe people are eagerly waiting for us to notice them and let them love us. **I seek safe people.**

Day 173

Perceiving

I differentiate what a person is available for and what they are not available for. People usually tell us what they can and can't do early on in a relationship. This is one of the wonderful features of human beings. People clearly express who they are without reservation right up front. The problem is that we women often hear what we want to hear. Then we are surprised and let down when a person can't show up, even if they told us from the beginning! For our own peace of mind on down the line in a relationship, it is imperative that we really listen to what someone says at first. We need to respect what an individual can and can't do to determine if this person is a match for us. While no one person can fulfill all of our needs and it is unfair to expect anyone to meet all our criteria, we are entitled to have reasonable expectations of a partner. Knowledge is power. Today, with a set of balanced expectations, we listen as a potential partner tells us about their availability. **I notice what a person can and can't do in partnership.**

Day 174

Contentment

I let myself be satisfied with a person. When we are stuck in our issues, we are usually dissatisfied. There is never enough. We always want that elusive "more" to complete us. We are unused to the feeling of satisfaction and immediately want to run away from someone who fills us up. Allowing ourselves to be contented by being with an emotionally available person may feel extremely uncomfortable. We fear them and question what's wrong with them. We look for the flaw that will disqualify them. Are they too boring, too patient, too sedate, too much in love with us? As we heal from our partnership issues, we learn it is important to sit with that feeling of satisfaction when we feel fulfilled by a person. We were put here on earth to be pleasured. Now we know that this is our opportunity to let satisfaction in via an available partner, even if this causes us discomfort. **I savor the feeling of contentment from being with someone who really satisfies me.**

Day 175

Impropriety

I notice when others are inappropriate. What designates inappropriate behavior? Each of us needs to create our own list of what we consider inappropriate. Some basics do apply, though. Examples are: yelling, criticism, mixed messages, emotional outbursts, any touch that we do not want, and lies. For each of us our list will differ in what we uniquely consider inappropriate behavior in a potential partner. Once we have our list, the next step is to notice when someone is inappropriate in these ways or in other ways which are important to us. Now if we notice that a person can't meet our expectations, we can let go of them. Does this mean we are looking for perfection? Will we deny ourselves a good person because they are not 100% at all times? Obviously the answers to these questions are "No." Extreme thinking sets us back; however, noticing inappropriate behavior in an individual helps us release an incapable person sooner. Then we move on to someone who is wonderful and appropriate for us. **Today I choose a person who is appropriate for me.**

Day 176

Appropriate Trust

I trust those who are trustworthy. If someone is married, cheating, lies to us, sends mixed messages, or in any other way gives us a signal that they are untrustworthy, we honor the facts. If an individual consistently displays that they are trustworthy, we take that into account and value their abilities. It may feel familiar to get wrapped up in a person who is somehow sly or shifty; however, this urge is only a manifestation of our own partnership issues. Doing research on who is trustworthy, and who is not, is necessary as we heal. We have to get out there and mingle. Interactions with potential partners, though, can be challenging for us. Doing research like this takes practice and patience. The upside is that we are steadily getting better and better at recognizing who is worthy of our trust and who isn't. Today we rely on ourselves to determine who we can trust. Then we act accordingly to let trustworthy people in. **I value a person who is trustworthy today.**

Day 177

Getting Close

I let safe people get close. Our yearning for intimacy is not chance. We yearn to connect with safe partners because we are made to love. The desire to flee an available person, however, signals that we are feeling a feeling we do not know how to process or that we are in a situation that is making us uncomfortable. Obviously some people will not be safe or desirable for us to interact with; however, if someone is appropriate for us and we are attracted, then the urge to run from intimacy is telling us something. Now we see that whenever we want to run away from another person because we are scared to death to get close, we are being invited to move deeper into ourselves. Inside of us is our spiritual self who knows how to and wants to give love. By moving into our feelings, learning to process our feelings, dealing with the core issues inside of us, and choosing situations where we are comfortable, we heal our partnership issues. No matter what the issue, by heeding our own signals we have a chance to move closer to ourselves. **I reveal my essence when it feels right.**

Day 178

My Natural Partner

I choose to be with my natural partner. Our natural partner is someone with whom we experience ease and a positive flow of energy. Things generally go smoothly with the partner we are naturally made to love. They treat us well, respect us, and are kind. They are not perfect; however, they do make an effort to amend behavior that we find distressing. They are available and show up for the relationship. We feel good in being around them. With our natural partner, we are able to maintain our identity while having the room to get and give the nurturing we need within the partnership. Going through this process helps us to find the knowledge of our natural partner. Once we know what we need in partner, we then practice being the lover we need in order to attract our natural life-mate. With time and practice we begin to embody the qualities of our natural partner. We start to love ourselves as we want our natural partner to love us. Then we find that there are many people who fit our description. A loving individual is out there waiting for us; doing this work brings us closer to lovingly throwing our arms around them. **I attract someone who reflects my self-love, my natural partner.**

Day 179

Alignment

I align my thinking with my desires.

"You are your only master, who else?"—The Buddha

When our backs get out of whack, we go to a chiropractor; when our tires need rotating, we go to a mechanic; when we need a job, we go to a recruiter. Connecting with the unavailable type is about being out of whack; there is a disconnection between our thinking and our desires. We convince ourselves with our mind to ignore our partnership desires in order to control the alignment; however, this never works. Healing our relationship issues is about honesty and courage, taking the appropriate actions to get closer to the integral helper inside of us who doesn't need to control anything. To fully honor our own desires means to accept what **we** want in a partner. Then once we accept our own needs, we reach true alignment in love. **Today I go to the master, my Self, in order to align what I think to what I desire.**

Day 180

Nurturing

I choose people who nurture me. I do it for fun. Choosing a partner who is nurturing takes a real commitment for us. We may be so used to being neglected and/or abused that the idea of letting in a person who is kind and considerate seems like an impossible ideal for us. The more we affirm that we love to connect with nurturing people, though, the more that will progressively become true. The more practice we get pretending that we are attracted to those who nurture us, the more we will naturally be attracted to those types of people. Today we know that "acting as if" we are attracted to loving, non-abusive individuals puts us on the road to healing. As we get our experience choosing available, non-abusive people, we see that it feels good to be with someone who loves us. Every one of us deserves love and nurturing. The wonderful news is that there are many potential partners out there who want to love a woman just like us. **Today I "act as if" I love to connect with nurturing people.**

Day 181

Competition with Other People

I refrain from competing with other people.

"My partner was a sprinkler-head, checking out other women all the time; and I just couldn't deal with it."—Kara

We deserve a person who appropriately gives us their attention; however, we often choose people who flirt with other people. We may choose these individuals because we believe there is a scarcity of quality partners available to us; we figure we have to endure this type of treatment. But this is not true! If we feel mammoth jealousy, envy, or fear when we are with our partner, we are being signaled that our partner is not treating us as we want. It is important to notice our feelings when we are out with our partner. Does this mean we will never get jealous? No. But to get important information about how we experience potential partners, we must practice being around others with them. We may not be able to engage with a potential partner and other attractive individuals at first because it may be too scary. That is fine. Wherever we are is OK. However, now we know that we get a lot of information about a person when we do. Even though it is terrifying, soon we see that people who are available to us can have "eyes for us" while being polite to others. No matter what happens, today we investigate without fear. **Today I choose a person who has eyes for me and treats other attractive people with interest and respect.**

Chapter Summary: At this point you are getting much better at identifying signs of emotional unavailability in others. You have a solid list of characteristics that are red flags. Your awareness is heightened when you date; you are learning to trust your own instincts. You are also starting to notice how you have pushed away available individuals in the past. Just remember to be kind to yourself. You are in exactly the right place. An emotionally available partner is waiting for you.

To conclude your work in this chapter, pick one person you have interacted with this month. Write a list of 3 characteristics that suggests they are available. Identify 2 people from your past who were unavailable. Make a list of the red flags they displayed. Imagine what an emotionally available partner would look like. (Imagine the physical, mental, and financial characteristics of your ideal mate.) Make a drawing of this person if you like. Place it somewhere where you will see it every day. Affirm that this person is waiting for you.

Now whenever you meet someone new, determine their availability quotient. Just remember that no one will be 100% available; 80% is just fine. You also need only be 80% available. Having balanced expectations of yourself and of others is essential for moving on in this process because the next chapter deals with the tough stuff: facing challenges, dealing with feelings, and surrendering control. Balance comes in handy as you move deeper into emotional maturity.

Phase II Summary: Congratulations on finishing **Phase II**! You have made wonderful progress so far. You have come a long way. During this phase, you have gained an essential understanding of other people. You are ready to let in the love of an emotionally available partner.

At this point, however, you may feel that you are dating more unavailable people than ever. You might worry that you will never be able to truly love someone. You may wonder if you will ever be able to stay present with an available person. Do not worry! You are doing very well. Perhaps you are just more aware of your attraction to the unavailable type now. Maybe you are just seeing your patterns of relating more clearly since you are less "foggy." No matter where you are, trust yourself. You are in the perfect spot for healing your partnership issues.

Now that you are done with **Phase II**, you face the major challenge of **Phase III**—fully growing into an emotionally mature adult. This is tough. For years, you may have been labeling your partners as the ones with the problem. (I know that I did.) To heal, learning to handle love's challenges with grace is essential. Dealing with rejection, despair, grief, and pain with maturity can be done. The next chapter guides you through.

Phase III

♥♥♥

Emotional Maturity

·7·

Rejection, Grief, and

Other Challenges

Chapter 7 will assist you in dealing with the major challenges of emotional loving. Covering everything from rejection, shame, loneliness, and grief to fear of your biological clock, this chapter addresses the challenges of your journey. Even though this chapter deals with the hard stuff, each day is moving you deeper into emotional maturity and true love. Move forward with courage!

Day 182

Coping with Rejection

I know that rejection is not personal.

"When I meet a pretty girl and beg her: "Be so good as to come with me," and she walks past without a word, this is what she means to say: "You are no Duke with a famous name" But I see no gentleman escorting you...yet you smile.... "Yes, we are both in the right, and to keep us from being irrevocably aware of it, hadn't we better go our separate ways home?"—Franz Kafka

Rejection is not personal: that is the most important thing about rejection. Many of us have rejected someone we later grew to admire—then we have chided ourselves for letting them get away! Other people often experience the same situation. Everyone gets rejected. Rejection is based on so little—simply our perceptions at that moment. Both men and women get rejected; that is simply a law of nature. Today let's release our fear of rejection and experience all that life has to offer. Today we no longer need to send mixed messages or go our separate ways home with a potential partner. Even if they are not a Duke, we may kiss a frog and find a Prince. **I release my fear of rejection today and I experience life.**

Day 183

Fear of Loss

I am willing to be willing to be willing to walk through my fear of loss.
Loss scares all of us silly. We have lost relationships, loved ones, and
possessions. Life is full of loss. The thought of losing can immobilize
everyone. For us, walking through our fear of loss takes tremendous courage.
We have seen relationships slip away several times in our lives. Many of us
have had to endure major heartbreaks. Emotionally available people know
they must take the risk of losing. Emotional availability means opening
ourselves up to the possibility of not being able to maintain a partnership. We
have survived all the losses in our past; chances are we will survive any other
losses that **may** occur in our future. One day at a time, using the key of
willingness, we surrender our fears of loss. **Today I have the courage to
face my fear of loss.**

Day 184

Snide Comments

I identify and firmly reject all snide comments. Single women have a hard
time of it in our culture. Being single can almost seem like a disease people
don't want to talk about. Society makes the supposition that marriage and
partnerships are preferable to being single. We can receive barbs or even well-
meaning comments from family members and colleagues when we are single.
Sometimes people do it "in fun." Whatever the motive, these snide comments
can deeply wound us as we heal. We cannot control the sensitivity level of
others; all we can do is treasure ourselves and remember that we are sacred.
Accepting other people's limitations, taking note that they are not being
considerate, discussing the behavior with them if we feel it will be helpful, and
asking that comments about our partnership status not be made are all
options to deal with snide comments. Whatever course of action we take, we
realize there are many amazing women journeying with us. We are not alone.
Now we also know that marriage is not necessarily the "be all and end all" of
life. Where we are today is just fine. **Today I know that snide comments
about my partnership status are inappropriate.**

Day 185

Biological Clock

I trust that I am in exactly the right place. The ticking biological clock is a reality. It leads to tremendous anxiety for many women. For women exploring our partnership issues, it can seem like the Universe's cruel joke that we have to take even more time out to heal when our bodies earnestly signal we are ready to procreate. We are people who have many fears about partnership, however, that need to be worked out. On the other side of our challenges, we vaguely see the outlines of the amazing fruits waiting to be harvested when we let in an emotionally available partner. Doing this work does not slow us down. It is the opening to a whole, vast world—the open sesame to a genie's treasure. This process makes us wonderful parents when the time is right. Today we know that there are many ways to parent children, including fostering and adoption. Now we know that this healing work is ensuring a new world for our children; therefore, we trust that where we are is just fine. **Just for today, I surrender all worry about where I am in the process of healing my partnership issues.**

Day 186

Grieving

I face my grief so that I can let go of it. Old relationships that have ended are hard to let go of. We often hold on to the ways a relationship ended; the unavailable person who was so perfect for us if only they would have changed; or that opportunity we missed because of our own partnership issues. Denying grief will not make it go away. In fact, the grieving is a necessary part of healing. Today we grieve for that woman we were and still are sometimes. Allowing ourselves to feel the hurt heals us; then we can be done with it. Mourning the woman we once were helps us avoid staying stuck too long in the grief phase, too. Then we walk freely into the sunlight knowing fresh new love experiences are waiting for us. **I grieve for myself knowing that I am moving toward an emotionally available partner.**

Shame

I release all shame about my past partnerships.

"Sin was originally an archery term that meant 'to miss the mark.'"—Eric

Life's too short to hold on to shame. Shame doesn't do anything for us. Shame can arise in us even when we haven't done anything wrong. Sometimes it was dishonorable behavior that caused our shame; sometimes it was just the circumstances we were in. No matter what, we grieve for that girl and woman we were in the past. All of us are doing the best we can with the information we have at any given time. What we did made perfect sense for the person we were at that time. This is our chance to absolve ourselves of any past shame. By putting our female experience out to the world, we let go of shame because we see that we are not so different from other women. The process of bringing our experiences into light as a female collective empowers us. Every time we decide not to carry shame around with us, we are healing. We didn't do anything wrong; we simply may have missed the mark. Today we bravely let go of all shame. **I release myself from the bondage of my shame. Today I love every part of myself, including my past.**

Day 188

Sneaking

I look behind my sneaky behavior to learn its lesson. Today we know that we no longer have to sneak around in order to get what we need. Our desires are normal and healthy. It is OK to ask for what we need. It is OK to reclaim what is ours by right on this planet. Obviously we can never demand anything from another person; however, this may not be the relationship that is right for us if we consistently have to sneak to get our desires met. We can be sure we are stuck when we feel we have to act furtively in order to get what we need from someone, when we feel that if we don't steal an individual's attention in sneaky ways that we will not get the attention that we need and deserve, and when we cannot resist the temptation to be underhanded. Anytime we have an inescapable desire to sneak and covertly get what we need, we now turn our attention inward. **Today I no longer sneak around to get my needs met.**

Day 189

Amends

I make appropriate amends. Chances are that by the time we are healing our partnership issues we have amends to make to ourselves and to others. We have done things which harmed another person. Several guidelines help as we begin to make apologies. Talking to a third party before making amends helps us clarify how to approach the person we need to apologize to. We remember to put ourselves into the shoes of the person we are making amends to, as well. Revealing some things can hurt another person; that is why we are careful. Forgiveness is also essential to the amends process. An apology made too soon, or when the time is not right, can backfire on us. We need to fully forgive the other person and focus on our part. Most importantly, an apology is not enough. We need to act differently with them in the future. Amends require a change in behavior. Now we know that making appropriate reparations to ourselves and others frees us. As we release ourselves from the bondage of our past misdeeds, we may even find that some people from our past actually make amends to us! **Today I get clarity on the amends I need to make and go to people with consideration for all involved parties.**

Day 190

Transition Times

I am kind to myself as I transition into a relationship. Moving into a new relationship can stir many issues up to the surface. We may greatly desire to be in a partnership; however, transitioning into a relationship takes adjustment. Single status gave us many luxuries that we took for granted. If the person is someone with whom we see a good possibility for true intimacy and positive relating, we now make the decision to move into the relationship. Whether an individual calls us often, wants a lot of our time, or seems needy, we know that being in a new relationship mandates a time of adjustment for us. Sometimes we will need a reminder placed here or there of why we enjoy being with this person to reaffirm that we want to be in the partnership with them. Whatever action it takes, today we are kind to ourselves and to our partner as we relate. **I nurture myself as I move into a relationship.**

Ambivalence

I deal with my ambivalence. If we are feeling ambivalent about an individual, it does not mean that we are unable to love on a global level. Feeling ambivalence about a person signals that that we are not ready to commit, that we are emotionally shaky, or that the potential partner we are feeling ambivalence about is not the right individual for us. Whatever the ambivalence is telling us, any time that we feel confused about which direction to take with a person signals a wonderful opportunity to get closer to ourselves. Then we have a chance to see what is going on behind the ambivalence. Today we simply use the information coming from our Self. We abstain from beating ourselves up. Emotional availability knows that there is always time for us to make a decision. Now we understand that taking our time to figure out what we need and want leads us to a good relationship. **I know that my ambivalence is normal in the process of healing.**

Day 192

Comparisons

I let go of all comparisons. Comparing ourselves to other people can get us in trouble. Comparisons do nothing for us. Comparisons position us to be judgmental of ourselves and to slip back into the self-hatred cycle. Comparisons hurt us because we never have a chance to be right-sized. We are only better than or less than. When we compare ourselves to other people with a better career, a great marriage, or a happier childhood, we often fall into the pattern of thinking their lives must be easy. Then we feel that life is unfair. Today we let go of all comparisons. When someone seems to have it all, practicing happiness for their good fortune is the antidote to our self-pity. It helps us claim our good from an abundant universe, and helps us take our power back to reach our goals. **I see myself as equal to others today.**

Day 193

Worry

I release all worry. The antidote to worry is letting go; giving the problem less energy, and stepping into the solution of trust, faith, and love. This problem will get worked out in us. All the worry we engage in is just wasting our energy. Whether we are worried about our behavior, our biological clock, or not getting a date for Saturday night, letting go offers us the opportunity to let the solution in. Sometimes our culture projects worries onto us, giving us the feeling that we are in for it if we are not at least trying to find a partner. However, The extent to which we are worried about something equals the extent to which we haven't let it go. Today we know that letting go is the answer to all of our problems. Once we release our tight grip even a little, the solutions come. **I let go of all worry today.**

Day 194

Emotional Baggage

I release all emotional baggage.

"Love like you've never been hurt."—Anonymous

Boy that's heavy! Let it go! Let it drop! Release all that unwieldy material and all the hang ups about partnership, love, and relationships! Doesn't it feel good to move freely without all the heavy weight of year's worth of emotional baggage collected as we moved from relationship to relationship? Hatred, anger, resentment, cynicism, hopelessness—let go of it all. Emotionally available people know that traveling light is a skill. Today we practice traveling emotionally light. Now we know that we don't need to carry negative experiences and bad feelings anymore on our journey. We joyfully let go of it all. **Today I take a load off of myself as I surrender all excess baggage.**

Day 195

Parents

I interact with my parents as I want to.

"Parents always see us as little children, even when we are 50 years old."—Martine

Parents usually mean well, yet it can be challenging to interact with our parents around the issues of partnership. Our parents were expected to get married. Since most of them did what society dictated, they expect the same of us. In our generation, though, the rules changed. We may feel vulnerable around our parents today when mom or dad says, "Why don't you settle down?" "I really want a grandchild," or "When are you getting married?" We can feel tremendous pressure from our parents, in addition to the cultural pressure we feel, and what our body is telling us. Sometimes setting boundaries with parents or explaining to them in a non-emotional moment why hearing such comments is problematic for us can help. Whatever the situation with our parents, let's remember we are not alone in having to confront our parents. Whatever course we decide to take with them, today we answer to ourselves. **I release my parents, and I do what I need to for myself around relationships.**

Day 196

Self-Hatred

I abstain from self-hatred. Self-hatred is very powerful and ancient in most of us; the desire to beat ourselves up usually started early in our lives. When we were little, we used self-hatred to explain the inexplicable. If a significant person, like a parent, abandoned us or hurt us, we assumed we had done something wrong. The practice of self-hatred developed as a desperate attempt to create a different outcome. We learned that we couldn't change other people's behaviors, but we could change our own. We believed that if we just acted differently, or better, then others would love us. Now we realize that the tool of self-hatred can't change anyone else's behavior. It can't make a person change, make them love us, or even make us never choose another unavailable person again. In fact, the only power that self-hatred really has is to show us that our issues have kicked up again. The real power of self-hatred is as an indicator that we are experiencing an uncomfortable feeling or are in some uncomfortable situation. Looking behind the distraction of self-hatred now helps us to see what is really going on. Then we let go of the behavior. **Today I realize that self-hatred can't change anyone else's behavior, so I gratefully let go of self-hatred.**

Day 197

Resentments

I let go of all resentment. Emotional availability is about telling someone how we feel when we don't know how they will react. Whenever we notice ourselves having conversations in our heads rather than with the person we are envisioning, we can be certain that we are holding onto a resentment that is limiting our ability to love. Stuffing our feelings doesn't help our relationship; it hurts us. The big draw to "milking a resentment" in this way is that we do not have to go out on a limb and share our hurt feelings with someone. The confrontation we are having in our minds is imaginary, not real. There is no chance for getting laughed at or told we are "making a mountain out of a molehill." When holding onto hard feelings, though, we miss the opportunity to clear the air with our partner and work out the issue. The magic of this healing process is that it helps us to tell the truth with integrity and dignity. When we do that, we let go of resentments at the same time. **Today I process my resentments. I speak truthfully to my partner.**

Day 198

Tears

I know that my tears are healing.

"If you cry tonight, you will look beautiful tomorrow."—Petra

Tears actually sedate us and make pain pass quicker. Wherever possible, it is best for our health to let ourselves cry our tears. As we cry, we get all the emotional energy out of us. Healing is not a quick fix. The process may bring us to tears many times. On our journey, we have lots of love experiences to grieve in a fresh way. Tears are a natural part of the process. If we find ourselves crying more than usual and with a greater intensity as we heal, this is normal. The process we are journeying through is significant. We can trust that we are right on target. Although we may be red and puffy now, we will look rested and beautiful tomorrow if we sleep on it. That is the power of tears. **I honor the natural power of tears today.**

Day 199

Bitterness

I release all bitterness. Many women in our culture are jaded about partnership. We have experienced difficult interactions with people that seem to reflect the negative cultural fictions about relating. These ideas include believing the hype that women are in the "one down" position in relationships or that there are only a few good potential partners left. For our own healing, it is important now to let go of bitterness because "people can't commit," are "only after sex," or are "inconsiderate." Believing that potential partners are problematic will ensure that we come into contact with individuals who exhibit these qualities. We no longer want that! Now as we make progress, we find that many wonderful, available, kind people exist in our communities waiting to be noticed. Actually those we are encountering are merely symbols of **our** consciousness. No one is perfect; however, making potential partners into villains is absurd. It is a generalization that negates true reality. Whenever something goes contrary to the way we want it to with someone, it may be very hard to see our part in the problem. To get clarity, friends can help point out **our** bitterness about partnership. Today we get the help we need. Everything is happening for a reason; sooner or later we will see the wisdom of every experience we have with partnering. Today we notice any movement into bitterness, and we courageously let go of it. **For the next 24 hours, I open myself to the idea that bitterness towards potential partners directly contrasts with the harmony available to me.**

Day 200

Over-Independence

I notice when I get over-independent. Independence is wonderful; however, sometimes we notice ourselves going to extremes. Over-independence is based on a lack of trust. We worry that our needs will not be met unless we do everything ourselves. We feel we must control every detail; we run ourselves ragged. The opposite extreme is to be overly dependent on another person. When we rely on another person completely, we abdicate our power. Either way we move makes us shaky. Today, we know that interdependence relieves us of these extremes. Interdependence is a principle based on sharing and giving that allows us as a society to rely on each other. Interdependence in a partnership allows each partner to give what they are able. Today maintaining our independence while acknowledging our interdependence on our partner yields a functional relationship. Now we get the help we need, when we need it. We notice when we get over-independent. **Today I am in balance because I am interdependent.**

Day 201

Trouble

I can face trouble with dignity and power. Many times on this journey we may slip and fall back into old behaviors. At such times it is easy to get discouraged. We may feel hopeless about resolving our partnership issues. We may feel embarrassed to continue talking about our shaky progress or the last time we "acted out" with a person. The miracle of our process is that whenever trouble comes knocking on our door, we get to answer with dignity and profound self-acceptance. We are very powerful beings living out a human experience. This journey is a spiritual experience in human form. Trouble only has the power to shake us up; it won't topple us. Today we are dignified and powerful as problems surface in our emotional lives. We know that every new day is a chance to practice. **Today if I experience trouble, I harness all my power to love myself and face my issues.**

Day 202

The Past

I release my past. Our pasts have generated a lot of regret that holds us back from moving on. Whether we acted out in sexually inappropriate ways with people or missed opportunities to connect with wonderful, available individuals, it is essential for us to review our pasts with compassion for ourselves rather than shame. One suggestion is to calmly look back at our interactions with past partners to determine areas we would like to amend. Seeing ourselves with this type of clarity helps us to locate patterns that need to be changed in us. Then we begin to trust that we are ready to let go of the past. Our pasts belong to us; therefore we review our pasts without shame or regret today. As a wise person once said, "Where we are now is exactly the right place." Today let's trust that we are on target. Let's love ourselves as we release our pasts. Then we can move on to a wonderful future with a loving, available person. **I review my past without shame or regret today. For this day I let go of my past.**

Denial

I am powerless over my partnership issues.

"Denial is not a river in Egypt."—Anonymous

Most of us have not wanted to admit our challenges; nevertheless, surrender is essential for progress. Being stuck doesn't make us weak or bad. When we are caught in the web of our partnership issues, we are only receiving a signal that we may need to go deeper into ourselves. By focusing inward, we then become whole, heal completely, recover our natural love abilities, and let in a wonderful relationship. Throughout this process of healing, many times we experience strong denial about our part in relationships that do not work out, interactions with people that are painful, and behaviors that confuse us. When we get emotionally shaky like this, it's usually easier for us to deny that we play a part; after all we are reading this book! Actually, as we progress in our healing, we learn that it is only by admitting that we are powerless over our partnership issues that we heal. Today, with great courage, we admit our relationship challenges. **If I find myself in denial, I acknowledge the truth.**

Infidelity

I am faithful. Many of us fear infidelity because our emotional shakiness may have led to our being unfaithful in past relationships; or we may have been cheated on by a partner who could not show up for us or for the relationship. Whatever our experiences in past partnerships, today we make a decision to walk through our fears of infidelity. Infidelity emerges for several reasons in relationships and is a reality; however, the truth is that many potential partners would not even consider playing false with a woman. If we are paralyzed from entering relationships because of our fears of disloyalty on our part or on the part of our partner, help is available. As we heal our issues, the need to cheat and the need to choose people who cheat, diminishes. Now we walk into safe relationships without fear and shame. **I know there are many faithful partners available to me.**

Day 205

Loneliness

I pay attention to my loneliness.

"H.A.L.T.S. Don't let yourself get too hungry, angry, lonely, tired, or serious."—Anonymous

Sometimes it seems like our loneliness will never end. When we get lonely, we have the chance to get close to ourselves. We are being signaled that we want to connect with another person in partnership. Our loneliness actually gives us more clarity about what we want; then we can take the steps to move toward a relationship. We can't control when we get into a partnership because we have no power over another person; however, acknowledging our need for human connection is powerful. In moments of loneliness, reaching out and doing service for other people can help. If we know someone who is having a hard time, we help them. Service takes us out of our loneliness and gives us the opportunity to feel useful; we also realize we are not the only ones hurting. It is important to notice how much we are really reaching out to others when we get lonely, because reaching out to others allows people to help us. Whatever tactic we take to assuage our loneliness today, we pay attention to the underlying desire to connect. When we start to take action in our behalf, the universe races to meet us. **I heed my own call by paying attention to my loneliness.**

Day 206

Issues/Problems in Relationships

I process challenges that arise in my relationship. Issues and problems come up in every relationship, functional or not. Part of emotional availability is processing issues and problems that surface in the relationship in a positive, effective way. Now as each and every issue or problem pops up in our partnership we ask ourselves three questions: "Why is this issue coming to my attention? What makes me uncomfortable with this problem? How can I look at this experience in a positive way?" When we get a sense of how we are reacting to the issue and a glimmer of what positive action we can take around the problem, we begin to act with more dignity, fearlessness, and compassion. Relationships are not easy. Partnerships take a lot of work. Now we know that examining our part, and determining to see the opportunity of every challenge, saves us from blaming our partner. **Today I fearlessly face the issues and problems in my relationship by asking myself three simple questions.**

Day 207

Holding On

I learn from my holding on to a person. Although we often hold on to another person in order to feel good about ourselves, holding on to someone else usually backfires on us. When we hold on so much and so tightly to an individual, we do not have a chance to relax and pursue our own interests. Everything becomes about binding this person to us. We fear that one day they will no longer be ours. Holding on is not about the moment, though; it is about scarcity. When we hold on we are trapped in fear and extremes. Now as we heal, whenever we find ourselves holding on, we know that our partnership issues have risen up. We tune into the message we are sending ourselves. The real goal of healing is to trust that a person wants to be with us as much as we want to be with them, to know we deserve a good partnership in our lives, and to be relaxed in the present moment. Today we find that if we let a person go even a little, we will see that they want to be with us. In order to get free, we make friends with our pattern of holding on so tightly to others. Then we are released from bondage. **I know that my issues hold on for good reasons. Today I let them teach me.**

Day 208

Regret

I let go of regret. Regret is a very slippery place for us. In those moments that we are rummaging around in our pasts, we are not present. When we regret that we missed out on may good love opportunities in the past, many of us forget that even then we were often thinking, "Oh, if only I was back two years ago...." The truth is that satisfaction is always hard to attain unless we are in the moment. When we slip into regret, we are not present. Regret does nothing for us. We cannot go back to the past. The best thing to do when we feel regret is to notice we are feeling remorseful, and identify regret as a detour from resolving our issues. We reconnect to ourselves as soon as possible when we feel regret bubbling up inside of us. Then we move into the present moment and heal. Now we know that this moment is all any of us really have; it is a miracle. **Today I look within if I am slipping into regret.**

Day 209

Fear of People/Avoidance

Other people have no power over me. I am free. True healing is about reclaiming our power; when we are free, we are no longer being ruled by other people. Often we have many frightening experiences to look back on, though. Today if we notice we are choosing to sidestep an individual because of our old fears, we check in with ourselves. It is always OK to avoid a person; there is no right or wrong when we tiptoe around someone. If we are still running our lives by avoiding people, there is no judgment. Our fears of rejection, of acting out with potential partners, of other people coming on too strong, or of ridicule can stop us in our tracks as we practice interactions. Now we know that admitting our behavior is profoundly helpful. Often sharing what we are doing with someone else lets light into the situation. As human beings we have a right to protect ourselves; we also have a right to go anywhere that we want without fear. If we decide we want to go anywhere, and we are sure that we will not be acting out by connecting with an unavailable person, then we know we have enough power today to practice interacting with potential partners. **I notice if I want to avoid someone.**

Day 210

Rejection

I let go of my fear of rejection. Everyone gets rejected, refused, rebuffed, cast out, thrown back, and/or discarded at some time. It hurts and is painful, but rejection is part of life. The most important thing to understand about rejection is that the person doing the rejecting is only working on limited information. Rejection is not based on something personal about us; it is about the other person. It is a simple lack of perception on that person's part. We don't need to educate any person who rejects us or change their mind. Now we know that rejection ultimately means is that there is another wonderful partner waiting for us. Even though it may not feel good when we get rejected, today we actually thank all the people with whom it hasn't worked out. Then we move on to be happy with someone else—an emotionally available partner. **I move on to a new love opportunity when I face a rejection.**

Day 211

Negative Comments

I let go of all negative comments. Our society so highly prizes "coupledom" that being single can inspire derogatory comments. Even when we are in a couple, we may hear negative comments from others about our partner or our lifestyle choices. Whenever we hear a comment that casts our relationship status in a negative light, these inappropriate and even rude remarks can deeply wound us. On this journey, we learn that not everyone is capable of consideration. Today we practice acceptance of other people's limitations; even when we may feel very vulnerable about our relationship status. Setting boundaries, maintaining tender care of ourselves, and identifying that the person who speaks has the issues helps. Whether we ask that no negative comments about our partnership status be made, or just decide to treat the other person like an invalid with pneumonia, whatever course of action we take is just fine. Now **we** remember that where we are today is OK. **I identify and release all negative comments about my partnership status.**

Day 212

Making Waves

I am willing to make waves. Being emotionally available is about telling the truth even when we don't know how the other person will react. Emotionally available people know that everyone is going to be OK if waves are made, that the relation-"ship" will not sink. Often we have been afraid to make waves with a partner, though. We feared that speaking out might end the relationship. We have had many experiences that seem to indicate that truth telling causes problems and upsets. What we forget is that the people we were involved with in the past were often unavailable. We also fail to realize that we ourselves were less skilled than we are today. Now we know that speaking our truth heals a relationship that is capsizing. Honesty enables us to stay comfortable in relationship with an available person. Although making waves takes courage and patience, and we may need support in order to tell someone what we are truly thinking, with practice we get better and better. **Today I get the support I need to make any necessary waves.**

Chapter Summary: Dealing with the tough stuff takes a big commitment to your healing. At this point, take a moment to acknowledge your courage. Dealing with rejection, loss, remorse, and grief presents major challenges. You are doing a great job of healing your partnership issues! Although it is not always pleasurable to have to face up to emotional growth, you have taken a big step forward by facing the hard stuff.

Right now, notice 3 areas where you have new insight on yourself. For example: Do you cry more now? How do you handle your parent's comments about your relationship status? Have you forgiven yourself for your past? The most important thing to remember is to be kind to yourself; you are in exactly the right place. No matter what the answer to these questions, you are a miracle.

Although it is difficult to accept, your partnership issues are trying to help you. The issues hang on until you listen to the messages they are sending. Your issues with partnership are guiding you to a place of profound self-acceptance and emotional maturity. To clearly hear your internal guide, you need to rely on your feelings. The next chapter reveals how this emotional self-reliance always helps you listen to your Self. Then you let go of the unavailable type and choose an emotionally available partner.

·8·

Relying On Our
Feelings

In this chapter, you will learn how to use your feelings as a guide in intimate relationships. You will discover how to process your feelings effectively, how to listen to the messages you are sending yourself, and how to validate your partner's feelings. Be kind to yourself as you embrace your emotional being. Your feelings will take you to the rich partnership you crave.

Day 213

Feelings

I understand my own feelings. Women traditionally have been told that we are too emotional, hysterical, or over-sensitive. Today we become our own authority. Letting go of society's messages takes practice; however, it is worth the effort. Now we validate our own feelings. We glory in all of them, even the painful feelings. Feelings always pop up for a reason. In fact, feelings often lead us to concrete information about how we experience a situation or a person. Many of us already have a wonderful connection with emotion. When we are emotionally shaky, though, our feeling skills are taken to the extreme. We often feel our feelings well, but then run from these feelings. We immediately hop into obsession, an unfulfilling relationship, or relationship anorexia to distract ourselves from the intensity of our emotions. Today we no longer need to run. Now we know it is OK to experience all our feelings. We experience the vital skill of emotional intelligence by owning what we are feeling when we feel it. Now we know that our feelings are telling us something important. **I validate my feelings as I validate myself.**

Day 214

Movement

I move into my feelings. Moving closer to our emotional selves helps us to work through our feelings. When we get closer to our emotional body, we know ourselves more completely. But it can be challenging to get in touch with our feelings if we don't have a lot of practice. The good news is that we may engage in many compulsive behaviors that signal we are out of touch with our feelings. Some indicators we have shut down our feelings include: checking our personal email 50-100 times per day, engage in excessive fantasizing, or dialoging with others in our head.

The best way to feel our feelings is to do a "feelings check-in" twice a day where we get quiet for a moment. We ask ourselves if we are mad, sad, glad, or afraid. Then when we know how we feel, we respond to this subtle part of ourselves. For example, one woman checked in with herself and realized she was feeling sadness and anger at a man she was dating. She took the time to get centered and process her feelings. Then she took the appropriate action and told him he had hurt her. He felt badly that she was hurting, but told her he was not willing to change his behavior in the future. She then made the decision to release him and has since moved on to a very loving, fun, available partner.

Emotionally available people know that a movement into our feelings helps us as well as our partners, because when we are in touch with our emotional body we do not project **our** feelings onto another person. A movement into feelings is a movement toward greater self-responsibility and harmony. Feelings always give us information that we can use to help ourselves figure out what we need. Today we choose to settle into our feelings as we heal. **In this moment, I love to move into my feelings. I do it for fun.**

Day 215

Going through My Feelings

I get help to walk through my feelings. We need to figure out what will aid us as we process our feelings. Feelings can be extremely powerful and daunting to walk through. Today let's remember that none of us is alone; support for our process is available. Support is available in many forms: friends, a therapist, a women's group, family who understand, and even literature about the emotionally unavailable man. We are worth all the effort the process of healing takes. Today we don't hesitate to get the help we need to walk through our feelings. **Today I take care of myself by getting all**

the support I need as I move into my feelings.

Validating My Partner

I validate my partner's feelings.

"Emotional availability is about letting the other person have their feelings."—Jim M.

Being emotionally available is the capacity to help a person identify and benefit from their emotions. We learn how to do this by validating our own feelings. Feelings actually give us concrete feedback about how we experience life, and the emotionally rich life benefits us all. Many people in our society have been taught to stuff their feelings. As we heal we learn that we need to be very comfortable allowing ourselves to experience all of **our** feelings in order to validate another person's feelings. Self-validation can be a tall order as we heal our partnership issues; remember that we are getting better one day at a time. Perfection is not the goal; the process is what matters. We are all, as human beings, entitled to feel as we feel. We do not have to act on our feelings or the feelings of our partner; however, a gift we give to the person in our life is validating their right to have all their feelings. **Today I validate my partner's feelings.**

Tantrums

I guide myself through my own tantrum. When we don't get what we want, sometimes we throw tantrums. The disappointment of realizing we can't get what we want, when we want it, with a person or in relationships can cause a tantrum to begin within ourselves. The energy of a tantrum builds on itself; then we are swept away by it. We may have been taught never to display our feelings in this innocent way, or we may have experienced people caving into our desires when we did throw a tantrum. Now we know that staying with ourselves and holding ourselves as we go through our own tantrums is essential to healing. Instead of inappropriately unleashing the power of our emotions on others, or stuffing our own feelings deep within ourselves, this day we take our own hand through the experience. By being receptive to our own emotions, we become better able to identify how we feel about events in our lives. Now whenever we feel a tantrum coming on, we know that it is a great opportunity to love ourselves. **I am my own guide through any tantrum I feel building within me.**

Day 218

Overwhelmed

I process overwhelming feelings. We women contend with many demands every day. For those of us facing our fears of partnership, it is extremely hard to sit with overwhelming feelings. Sometimes we just need to "pull the plug." Leaving a relationship often seems like the answer. Abandoning someone is an extreme reaction popping up, though. We may have learned to cope in our lives by thrusting out relationships when we got overwhelmed; however, today we are adult women. We have the ability to walk through overwhelming feelings and to take care of ourselves. Feelings just exist. They are not a threat to our well-being. Feelings are emotional energy, and they do pass. With detachment and time, we effectively deal with our feelings. Today in that moment of overwhelm, we sit with our feelings. **Today I process overwhelming feelings.**

Day 219

Awareness

I increase my awareness of my feelings. Our feelings are trying to tell us something. Feelings never lie. Trying to control or stuff our feelings only works for so long. When we ignore our feelings, there is always a heavy price to pay for that type of denial; we devote ourselves to a person who cannot fulfill us. Now we build our self-esteem one day at a time, and sometimes one moment at a time, by checking in with ourselves gently. We ask how we feel about a person. Now when we mingle or date, we ask ourselves questions. We ask, "How am I responding to this person? Do I feel scared, mad, glad, or sad when I am around this individual? Am I irritated, excited, lonely, or energized by them? Do I feel comfortable?" When we get our emotional information, we are better at being true to ourselves. Since feelings are not of the material realm, it takes time to get used to listening to them. Each time we practice, we build faith in our power to take care of ourselves. Now we give ourselves the person we need because we are aware of our feelings. **I know**

my emotions always tell me the truth.

Day 220

Listening

I hear my partner's feelings. Active listening mirrors back to a person what we hear them say. When we actively listen to a potential partner, we give them a gift because we are present for them. The message we send when we truly listen to an individual and to all of their feelings is that they are important to us; however, part of what makes listening to a potential partner challenging for us is that our own needs become paramount in our minds. We may have trouble letting go of old resentments. We wonder why our partner won't listen to us!

In moments like these, it is helpful to remember that every one of us on this planet wants to be happy and loved; in fact, love is our birthright. When we honor a person today by hearing their feelings, we generate more love on Earth. Then the love will be returned to us; our needs will be met. Often our ability to be emotional and to process our feelings is what attracts people to us in the first place. Today we give another person the gift of listening as they experience their feelings. We bless them in this process and realize they are special. Healing is about giving. When we give, we are letting in an emotionally available person. **I listen as my partner shares their feelings.**

Day 221

Self-Validation

I validate my own feelings. Owning our own feelings gives us the chance to get closer to essential information that empowers us. Being emotionally available is about power. No one else is our authority. In the past we may have been told that our feelings were too intense, out of control, or shameful. Now we know that the only person who needs to validate our feelings is us. The process of healing gives us the opportunity to become rational, adult women around other people, relationships, and sex. We may have been told how to feel by society, by our parents, by our past partners, and even by other women; however, today is the day to reclaim our own power to self-validate. No matter what feelings we are feeling, even if they are not culturally approved, we are our own authority. By moving into our feelings, we give ourselves the chance to substantiate our experience as women. We get closer to ourselves, and we let in an emotionally available individual. **I am my own authority with regard to my feelings.**

Day 222

Feelings

I verbalize my feelings. Our partnership issues are about secrets, pretending everything is fine when we are dying inside, or expecting someone else to understand from our expression or body language that everything is not OK. A simple solution to the complex problem of trying to change **them**, though, is simply to speak out about **our** feelings when the time is right. Many of us never learned that feelings just exist; we weren't taught that feelings deserve to be shared. In past relationships we attempted to avoid sharing our feelings. Many of us even left partnerships in order to avoid sharing our emotions. Now we know that is not necessary. Each time we appropriately verbalize our feelings with our partner, it is a gift that we give to them and to ourselves. Now we know that the gift of honest sharing is an expression of ourselves. **Today I express my feelings verbally.**

Day 223

Anger

It's OK to be angry. We women have a right to our anger. We may have been taught that anger is unladylike, yet this idea is simply misinformation. Anger is just an emotion people experience. Though it has a powerful energy behind it, the emotion itself is not destructive. In fact, anger channeled positively can lead us to manifest many dreams. Anger acknowledged constructively is actually a great indicator that our boundaries are being crossed. It signals that we need to pay attention to what is going on inside, or outside, of us. Often our anger erupts because we are trying to deny that problems exist. Now we no longer have to deny our anger. Today we know that anger is powerful and helpful if processed correctly. When we notice that we are angry, we take the time to check in with ourselves and figure out what we need to do in order to heal. If we need help to manage our anger, we take an anger management course or get help from a professional. (See the Bibliography at the back of this book.) With assurance, we feel all of our feelings. **Today I process my anger in ways that help me.**

Day 224

Fear

I notice when I get in fear. Even though fear is "false evidence appearing real" and the opposite of faith, fear is a hard one for many of us. Sometimes we are in denial and don't even realize that fear is tyrannizing us. We deny that we are afraid. We may also go the other direction and attribute other emotions, such as excitement, exhilaration, or attraction to fear. What we forget is that fear is basically "forgetting everything's all right." Now if we notice that we are getting fearful, we have a better chance of actually staying present. If we get fearful of committing, and intimacy just seems too overwhelming, today we acknowledge the fear. Then we make friends with it. Fear has something to teach us. It is an emotion that wants to bring us into faith. Now by quietly and patiently examining our fear, we learn about ourselves. **I make friends with my fear as I learn to be in faith.**

Day 225

Shame

I release shame about my body. Women are taught to feel ashamed of our bodies and who we are throughout our lives. Many feminine products exist on the market to disguise our odors and help us control our weight, menopause isn't celebrated, and sexually we may have gotten the message that we are dangerous or unsightly. Today we let go of all this simple ignorance on the part of the mass market and stop our complicity in our own indoctrination. The process of releasing shame is not easy, yet it is possible. It begins for each of us as a thorough appraisal of what it means to be a woman. Committing to loving our bodies, seeing what our bodies do for us each day, loving ourselves as we are, at whatever age or weight we are, and exulting in ourselves as sexual beings frees us from shame about our femininity.

The female body is a miraculous spiritual force that allows us to bring new life into the world if we so choose, to endure more pain than men, and to feel sensual and sexual pleasure at any age or weight. Releasing the shame that has been taught to us allows us to truly move into who we are—wonderful women who deserve a partner who loves us unconditionally. Body shame is outdated; therefore, today we release it. Now we choose a partner who honors our body. **I let go of all shameful feelings about my body.**

Day 226

Empathy

I empathize with how my partner feels. Our partners have feelings too; they need to be understood and validated. Emotionally aware partners may seem few and far between, because people are often not well practiced at sharing themselves and their feelings. To truly love someone, though, means picking up on the subtle clues they give us that they are experiencing feelings. Whether they are hiding, glued to the remote control, shopping a lot, sucked into a video game, or seem only able to connect with their friends for a time, we let them be where they need to be without taking it personally. When they feel our acceptance, they may feel freer to share themselves and their feelings with us. No matter what they do, we get the chance to show another person how much we love them by empathizing with them. Empathy can be extremely difficult for us, for it may bring our own fears to the surface. For today, though, let's trust that an individual is with us because they love us. As we love our partner back, we are present and empathetic when they are ready to share with us. **I let a person share themselves as they are able.**

Day 227

Self-Empowerment

I honor and empower my spirit. Our spirit can get lost in the search for "The One." Neglecting our spiritual selves is a common trait in women who choose the unavailable type. Even if we have a solid spiritual belief, we may not have heard our spirit calling out to us. The focus on our appearance or with finding a partner may have taken precedence over our spirit in the past. Now, giving our spiritual self the respect it deserves means heeding our own call. Today is the day for us to get in contact with that still place inside. Now when we truly listen to our spirit; we seek a relationship with a person who pleases the spiritual part of us. We empower our spirit by testing types of people out, interacting with potential partners, and checking in with how we feel in being with an individual. Are we refreshed? Do we feel good? Are we happy? Do we feel spiritually fulfilled around this person? If the answers are

"Yes," we trust our Self. Then we build a relationship with an emotionally available partner. **Today I let my spirit guide me in the search for my natural partner.**

Day 228

Hope

I keep hope alive. This process may take time; however, it is working. When we are alone, suffering, or butting our heads up against the wall one more time, we may lose hope that we can truly change. Whenever this happens, we must remember that we do not actually need to change ourselves at all. All we have to do is release old protective behaviors that cover up our true selves. These behaviors no longer serve us. As we peel each layer of our behavior off like we would an onion, the things that cover over our true selves will be lifted. An onion has a strong odor, though. It can turn people off. It can also make us cry when we cut into it. Our healing process can be the same way. When we uncover a new layer of our healing, we may think, "I am just getting worse. I keep messing up." What this really means is that we have reached a new level of challenge. Now we keep the faith that we will learn new behaviors. Keeping our hope, trust, and faith in the process alive expedites our healing. With hope we cannot fail. **I keep the faith that I am healing.**

Day 229

Strife

I avoid strife and I seek peace. Peace is gently kind and feels good; it can also feel extremely strange to us. Because we are used to strife, drama, and struggle, the pull back into these feelings is strong. The choice of peace can seem inadequate. If we are legitimately angry or feeling many old fears surface in a relationship, peace may seem like the last place we can go. The re-conceptualization of problems in relationships as opportunities to move into healing helps us in these moments. Now we know that the solution to all strife is peace. As we heal, we start to believe that whatever we are experiencing in our relationships right now is exactly what we are meant to be experiencing. We learn that the problem is surfacing so that we have the opportunity to calmly and gently step into harmony. Today we know that stepping out of hurtful, problematic, intimacy-blocking strife makes peace possible. Now we choose the solution. **I step away from the problem and into peace.**

Day 230

Answers

I seek answers. Confusion can be tremendous for us. We may have trouble making decisions about potential partners, confusion about when to move into a relationship with a person, and difficulty discerning what we can accept and what we can't. Our feelings give us information, yet the strength of our feelings may overwhelm us. Our tendency to connect with the unavailable type functions as a race away from feelings and decision making. That is why many of us sought out people who would make our decisions for us or who made us feel a certain way. Today, we do not need others to deal with our feelings. We trust that the force of our feelings will pass. As the feelings leave, information is transmitted. If we stay with ourselves as we feel our feelings, than the answers are clear. Today we make our own wise decisions. Our answers are inside of us waiting to be excavated. Now we look inside for the answers. **For this day only, I arrive at my own answers.**

Day 231

Reliance

I trust my feelings.

"My feelings are the only thing I can trust."—Judy

Honoring our feelings is a revolutionary concept for us. It takes practice when our society is about cold hard facts. Feelings give us concrete information that something is going on at an emotional level with us, though. Often we may have no idea what triggered a feeling. Now if we get centered and clearly review our day whenever we experience a feeling, we find that the feeling exactly matches an experience from the past 24 hours. Now we review our day when we experience emotions.

Reliance on the subtle feelings inside of us also gives us treasured information that helps us make good decisions about a potential partner. Whenever we experience anger, depression, hopelessness, love, or joy when we are with someone, we are getting good information about how that individual works for us. As we interact with potential partners, the reliance on our feelings provides a wonderful tool to decide who is right for us. The more we practice, the sooner we enter an available relationship. **Today I rely on my feelings for information.**

Day 232

Going the Distance

I tolerate the feeling of satisfaction from being around a person for longer periods until I don't have to run away at all. We may not know how to let another person fulfill us. The discomfort of being fulfilled in a relationship can send us running. We pout, yell, run away, or nitpick. Shutting down like this is not wrong; however, it can wreak havoc in our relationships. Now when we notice that we are cut off from our feelings, we calmly return to being present in our bodies.

Even though it takes courage to stay with our feelings about a partner, especially if this person is satisfying us, with practice we can tolerate the feeling of satisfaction with a person for longer periods of time. We find that we don't have to run away from them at all! Our partnership issues may pop up from time to time; however, now we are so clear in ourselves and our healing process that we trust our ability to return to our partner. A reliance on the tools that have worked for us in the past serves us in the future: checking in with ourselves without judgment, and listening to what our feelings have to tell us. Often when we sit with the feelings of satisfaction in being with a person, we find that there are several potential partners who are just right for us. Our issue has been healed. **Today I love the feeling of satisfaction being around another person gives me.**

Day 233

Attention

I get my own attention. Healing our partnership issues means showing up for ourselves and paying attention to our own call. Any detours into compulsion or obsession, extreme anger, hatred, rage, or irrational fear are great indicators that we are in need of attention. Our strong emotions are not here to torture us, though. Actually they are signals that we need to get back in balance.

It hurts when our expectations of a person are not met; however, today **we** are sensitive to our own needs. We do want a partner who pays attention to us; yet we know that healing is not about finding a person to fill the hole in us. Now we get our own attention and hold it. Then we are able to let someone give us their attention because we are so used to being showered with love and care. Taking this one step further, we next develop the ability to give away the abundance of what we have to our partner. That way the love builds and builds. **Today I shower myself with love and attention.**

Day 234

Empathy

I empathize with how I feel. As we heal, we are discovering that it's hard and it hurts sometimes to be on this road. At other times it is joyful and fun. Sometimes we feel alienated and left out, or that we are being punished; at other times we feel gratitude and wonder at how joyful we feel. This process means truly getting close to our all of our feelings. It entails giving ourselves the acceptance we need when we are emotional. Today, using all of our intellectual understanding, we relate empathetically to our feelings. We hold ourselves with love and care, no matter what feelings pop up. Empathy is the intellectual identification with our feelings. Now, whenever we notice that we are cut off from our feelings, we use all of our faculties: emotional, spiritual, and mental. **I relate to all my feelings today.**

Day 235

Sudden Emotional Withdrawal

I respect my emotional withdrawals. If we experience sudden emotional withdrawal as we get close to an individual, we know that our partnership issues have kicked up. Often getting close to a person will trigger a tremendous fear of intimacy in us; therefore sudden emotional upheavals are normal. Many women act out by causing a fight, flirting with other people, giving someone the silent treatment, not returning phone calls, resuming a pointless argument, or pouting.

Whatever forms our issues take, the best thing to do is not to panic or assume that the person we are with is the problem. Taking a deep breath, we move closer into our emotional body. When we want to pull away, we see what is going on inside **us**. Our process of recoiling from a person usually signals that we are feeling powerfully. Taking the time to get quiet, centered, and self-inquisitive leads us to the answers we need. Now when we notice our sudden withdrawals, we thank our issues and get the support we need. **Today if I notice my sudden emotional withdrawals, I move deeper into myself.**

Day 236

Jealousy

I let go of jealousy today.

"I have never understood jealousy. Being attracted to someone is such a gift that, if I focus on that, I have no reason to be jealous."—Hillary Flye King

Jealousy is a very challenging emotion; it is the green-eyed monster. To let go of jealousy often takes a lot of practice. Conceptualizing attraction as a precious gift helps us. Now we know that if we honor our attractions, jealousy is irrelevant. If we love someone we can return that strong emotion whenever jealousy rears its head. Feeling jealousy means we decide that other women are a threat to our relationship with a potential partner, we believe in scarcity, and we assume everyone else has already taken all the good people.

Being gentle with ourselves along the way helps whenever jealousy rears up. Our jealousy signals that our issues have a message for us. It is always OK to feel jealous; the important question to ask ourselves is how that jealousy feels and what it is trying to teach us. Keeping the focus on ourselves and on our own feelings of attraction, where our attention belongs, defuses our jealousy. Now we know that attraction is a divine gift to be celebrated. **If I notice I am feeling jealous, I keep the focus on me. I release my jealousy.**

Day 237

Humility

I am humble. When we are driven by our partnership issues, we are proud and immodest. Now as we awaken to our past behavior, we may feel humiliated. We clearly see how our ego has revolved around partners: getting them, getting away from them, blaming them, begging them for attention, our inability to be friends with them, or controlling them. Our relationship fears have brought us low many times.

But humility does not equal humiliation. If we slip into humiliation as we face the power of our issues, then we need an antidote. Humility is always the antidote to the arrogance of our ego. Humility is an understanding of our right size. While everything in our culture teaches us that to be meek is to be weak and lowly, today we know that humility is different than humiliation. The extreme humbling that our partnership issues have given us helps us to be teachable. Then we are able to let real love in. **For the next twenty-four hours, I practice humility.**

Day 238

Harmony

I release all bitterness and choose harmony with a partner. Harmony means peacefully co-existing with and complementing the person in our lives. Being in harmony means that the energy radiating out from our partnership is full of love. Although most of us have rarely been in harmony with our partner for long, harmony is our birthright. We are loving beings whose essential nature is love; however, we have often treated our partners with antagonism or hostility instead. To let go of all of our relationship fears means getting back to the basics of what we already know how to do intuitively, which is to love. Today let's trust ourselves, because love is about harmony. Now we promote love on a daily basis by releasing bitterness, being harmonious with ourselves, and loving the person in our lives. **I am in harmony with my partner, which is the exact opposite of bitterness, for the next 24 hours.**

Day 239

Anger

I appropriately express and take responsibility for my anger.

"Anger is a secondary emotion. It is just a cover for pain."—Anonymous

Anger is a powerful emotion. Sometimes we are scared of our own anger. We may have "stuffed" it for years or let it out at inopportune moments. If we grew up around raging parents or other angry adults, we may have experienced anger as pathological. We now may fear that we have a disease passed down from them whenever we feel angry; however, anger is simply an emotion. Only our behavior can actually cause harm.

Today our goal is to honor our anger. Anger is a powerful energy signaling that we are hurt. If we "stuff" the anger, we are not allowing ourselves to acknowledge our own pain. Harnessing our anger effectively instead, we use it to heal. Ways to harness our anger proactively include tearing up an old phone book, kickboxing, or pounding a pillow.

Whatever way we handle our anger, we also realize that our anger means we need to listen to what's going on. Anger tells us that our boundaries have been crossed; it means that a limit we set is not being respected. Now we know that taking responsibility for our anger means we have the opportunity to get close to that part of ourselves that needs attention. Once we know why we hurt and have clarity about what our anger is telling us, then we wait until we are calm before we clearly communicate our feelings with our partner. **Today I honor my anger. I respect my emotion as a signal that I am hurting.**

Day 240

Rebounding

I am aware of my process if I choose to rebound from a relationship. When recovering from a break-up, some of us tend to rebound. By rebounding we are thrown into the rush of a new relationship. Then, it seems as if we don't need to process our feelings for a person. Actually the rebound is a distraction from our issues with that person we are running from; the issues won't go away even though the rebound may feel good in the moment. If we need or want to rebound, that is always OK. If we choose to rebound, though, we can be sure that the issues from our past relationship will surface again. Rebounding can be a movement out of emotional balance, but ultimately we are our own authority. There is no judgment about what we women "should" do when letting go of a relationship. Today we become aware of our own style so that we get what we need as a relationship ends. If we take the rebound route at the end of a partnership, we get a chance to see how rebounds feel for us. **Today I stay present with myself if I rebound from a relationship.**

Envy

My envy is teaching me about what I want. Envy is a trait that differs from jealousy. Envy is characterized by the desire for some advantage another possesses, while jealousy is feeling resentment against someone else because of their advantage. Many of us have the tendency to become envious if another woman is engaged, married, or a mother. What envy signifies is that we desire to be in her shoes. Whenever we experience strong feelings in connection with a woman or a man who has what we want, today we have the opportunity to get clear on whether it is jealousy or envy working in us. If jealousy is popping up, we work to let the resentment go and try to be happy for that person. If envy is at play, then our real work is to acknowledge that we sincerely want what she/he has; then we go to any lengths in order to obtain what we envy.

Emotional availability does not appear by magic in most people; relationships take work even for those to whom love seems to come easy. If someone has what we want, we ask them how they achieved it, we practice new behavior, and we cultivate the willingness and ability to do the necessary footwork to get it. Doing the work will not guarantee we will get what **they** possess; however, it will lead us to **our** healing. **I release all envy. I go to any lengths to get what I want.**

Shutting Down

I abstain from shutting down around a partner. Staying present with another person takes a lot of practice and self-awareness for us. Letting go of our judgments about how relationships should play out, who we should be attracted to, and the willful control we have hung onto for dear life is necessary. This is a tall order for many of us. If we trust the process, however, we will not fail. Today we are more present and remain that way. Our decision to avoid shutting down gets us back into our bodies and into our feelings sooner. Now we learn amazing lessons about ourselves as we identify the triggers that cause us to dissociate around potential partners. We stay present for ourselves and for our partner. **As I stay aware around another**

person today, I gain faith that I will be taken care of in the long run.

Day 243

Emotional Maturity

I have the emotional maturity of an adult woman. Focus on our positives takes practice. Each day we do many things well because we are skilled, capable, and adult. In relationships, our skills can be tested. We may act inappropriately by pouting or yelling. We may shut down with our partner by being surly or uncommunicative. We may run away from the relationship. Knowing our own skill level, and accepting where we are, is important as we work through our fears. If we need a crash course, a growth workshop, or just some practice in intimate relationships, today we get the experience and help we need. We also pat ourselves on the back for how far we have come. Today we note all the tremendous progress we have made on this path. Healing is a process, not a magic act. We are now emotionally mature enough to honor this moment. There is no judgment, shame, or blame involved in examining our skill set in intimate relationships. We have only the sincere desire to get better and better. **I realize how emotionally mature I am.**

Chapter Summary: Feelings give you important information about your reactions to potential partners. Although you may not have been taught to stay with your feelings, turning your attention inward will help you heal your partnership issues. At this point you are realizing that you are up to the challenge. Now you are beginning to see that accessing your feelings just takes practice. You are also learning that listening to your feelings teaches you to be emotionally empathetic with a partner. That way you can have the emotionally rich partnership you want.

To get a sense of your progress, list 3 feelings you had today. Were you angry, sad, scared, or happy? Can you relate those feelings to events that happened today? Are you only feeling "blah?" If so, that's OK. Now you know that all your feelings are worthy; no feeling is more valid than another. Also answer these questions: Did you listen to what another person had to say in the last week? Did you affirm their right to have feelings? Did you stop yourself from taking your partner's feelings personally this month?

Give yourself a pat on the back for all your progress! At this point you are becoming very powerful. You are starting to hold your emotional self with love and care. You remember that your feelings always manifest for a reason. You know that your emotional energy will pass.

The only place that you may get tripped up is when you notice that some of your feelings are hard to handle. If you feel overwhelmed; this is normal! If you need some assistance to deal with your feelings, there are many types of support available, including therapy and women's groups. (See the Bibliography for ideas.) Remember you are not alone.

You have been using painful relationships to hide from the true pain of your feelings for a long, long time. It is scary to uncover the raw emotions under your surface, but remember that feelings are your friends. No matter how challenging dealing with feelings is, be kind to yourself on your journey. Your own self-support is essential. It sustains you as the next chapter takes you to the highest level of emotional maturity—giving up control.

·9·

Letting Go of

Control

Chapter 9 will increase your ability to give up control in intimate relationships. You will learn how to embrace your behavior with others, how to abstain from trying to change people, and how to legalize all potential partners. Letting go of control is the most difficult part of emotional maturity, but you can do it! Each release of control will bring you closer to a wonderful life-mate who can meet your needs.

Day 244

Control

I let go of control.

"With all the energy I have directed into trying to control potential partners and obsessing on them, I could probably have been President of the United States!"—Carolina

Holding the reins on people takes energy and power that we could be using in healthy ways, it doesn't feel good, and it can only be done for so long. Because holding on has seemed to be the only way for us to feel safe, though, letting go of control can be very unsettling. What most of us don't know is that letting go of control does not mean that we give up our power; in fact, healing teaches us that we have the ability to do all the necessary footwork to get our needs met. But ultimately we know that the results are not ours to control. Emotionally available people know that letting go opens the hands to receive. It gives us the choice to let in all the love that's available in the universe. Today we let go of ruthless control that doesn't give us the ultimate satisfactions we desire. Now we try something else: letting go of control and surrendering to the process knowing we will get what we need. **I am comfortable letting go of control.**

Growth

I am growing emotionally mature.

"Growth is the opposite of control."—Anonymous

When we hold on so tight, we are not growing. Whenever we need to be right, need to feel in power over what is happening to us in our partnership, or need to control our responses to our partner, that is a sure sign that our issues have popped up. To heal we need to grow; however, the only time we grow is when we let go of control around partnership. It can seem exceedingly scary to many of us to let go of control, because growth is painful. Most of us have never fully grown up, so the growing pains of being emotionally mature present major challenges. Many of us still act like adolescents around potential life-mates. That small part of us is balking all the way whenever we attempt new ways of emotionally relating to a potential partner. Today we do not give up, though. We know that we are getting better with each release of control. We are becoming emotionally available. **I let go of control and choose to grow.**

Changing My Behavior

I completely let go of the goal of changing my behavior around potential partners. As we get clearer about our own emotional issues and healing, self-observation of our behavior is invaluable. We see that our behavior always makes perfect sense, even if it mortifies us or confuses us. If we are running away from available people, choosing people who hurt us, or are taking on too many commitments to have a relationship, we stop trying to change. This does not mean that our behavior is always desirable or effective in the scope of our long-range goals; however, today we make the decision to observe our own behavior without changing it. Now we know that no matter how we are acting around people, all behavior is OK.

For example, if we get upset and overreact when the one we love lets us down slightly, we ask ourselves if we are trying to make it easy to end the relationship. Was our partner's behavior really so upsetting that we want to avoid the good parts of the partnership? A wise person once said, "You can't say the wrong thing to the right person." Even if we fear we will drive a potential partner away or will limit our chances of ever having a relationship, we make the courageous decision to abstain from changing our behavior around other people. We develop the faith through experience to know that as we gain awareness our behavior is amended naturally when the time is right. Then a wonderful partnership appears. **In this moment, I know that my behavior is just fine.**

Day 247

Authority

I legalize all behavior around potential partners. Resolving our partnership issues means that we accept all of our behavior around other people. Remember: you can't say the wrong thing to the right person. As we heal, we look at our behavior as if it were a science experiment. When we find our behavior doesn't match our goals, we acknowledge the behavior. Then we gently query why we would act in a way which doesn't serve us. The process is not about judgment; it is about information. If we find we are acting silly, morbid, attention starved, or high and mighty with potential partners, we may be tempted to beat ourselves up. The antidote to this is affirming that we love all our behavior around other people. Self-affirmation exhibits true self-compassion. As we progress, even if we find that we do not like our behavior around people, we soon see that all our behavior is OK. If we find that we sincerely **want** to change a behavior that we find ineffective, then we get the help necessary to let go of it. We may make mistakes as we walk this path; however, now we know we can't say the wrong thing to the right person. **I am my own authority today. I give myself permission to engage in all behavior around potential partners.**

Day 248

Changing My Partner

I abstain from trying to change my partner. Today we choose a partner who appeals to us. If we see that a person has many characteristics that we would like to change, which irritate us, scare us, or turn us off, we can examine our motives in being with them. Are their quirks really too much for us or is it just easier to look at their peccadilloes than to take care of our own lives? Are we acting out of low self-esteem? Are we feeling unworthy of a whole and actualized partner? Are we afraid to focus on our own healing? Do we seek a lower companion so that we will look good in comparison to them? Changing ourselves takes a lot of energy. If we are taking a person we may feel is "damaged goods, yet full of potential," we may want to sit for a while and get clear on our motives. Today we choose to work on ourselves. Now we pick from among the abundance of wonderful, actualized, and acceptable people in order to let love in. **I choose a partner I do not have to change.**

Day 249

Obsession

I can obsess on a person any time I want. It is always OK. Knowing it is always OK to obsess leads us to a profound place of self-trust. If we cannot let go of a preoccupation, we know that it is OK. Obsession is a very ancient, powerful tendency in most of us. Sometimes the pull to excessively focus on someone is too powerful to surrender. Today we are gentle with ourselves if we are drawn into an obsession. Setting a five-minute boundary on what is haunting us is a tool that often quiets us. If the preoccupation is persistent, though, looking behind it reframes obsession as a wonderful teacher. Obsessing on a person means that we are in an uncomfortable situation or are experiencing an uncomfortable feeling. Now we have the magic opportunity to use our preoccupations to get closer to ourselves. When obsession hangs on powerfully, we move into our feelings to discover what is really going inside. We use obsession to take stock of our lives. No matter where we are in our journey to release obsession, we are just fine; we are going to make it. This process is about self-love. It is about giving ourselves the permission let go of control and be who we are in this moment, no matter what. **I love myself, even if I am preoccupied with someone else.**

Day 250

Discomfort

I am natural when I am with a potential partner. Nature is pure and sacred. So are we. Our natures as women are beautiful and profound. We have often denied our natures, though. Now, as we heal, it can be uncomfortable and scary to allow ourselves the permission to be natural around another person. We feel that if we let ourselves go we will be devouring monsters with a deep well of need, we fear we will be overly submissive and timid, or we worry we won't be able to maintain a sense of self in relationship. Many of us are exceptionally gifted at controlling our natures based on such fears, but nature cannot be controlled for long. Our partnership issues actually function as a signal that we are not being natural; therefore, learning to heed our own signal that something is wrong is central to healing. Whenever we shift into control mode or are in excessive fear, we know it is time to check in with our feelings. Then we take the further step of being who we are with someone else, which is beautiful. **I respect myself and withstand the discomfort of being natural with another person.**

Day 251

Tranquility

I make total peace with my behavior around potential partners. No matter how we act around a person, it is OK. If we feel we have put our foot in our mouth, if we get excitable, or if we get spacey, every behavior is acceptable. All of the behaviors we engage in around potential partners are acceptable. For us, making peace with our behavior can feel extremely uncomfortable. We want to be loved. Our fear is that if we are not at least trying to control our behavior, we are doomed of ever finding a partner. By acting like we "should," though, we are not showing people the truth. Sooner or later, we cannot handle the pressure of denying ourselves. Denial never works for long, and we deserve to be ourselves in relationships. Who we are without any artifice is just fine. If we are not attracting as many people as before, this is normal. This simply means that we are getting closer to attracting the individual we will be fulfilled by—the person who wants to be with **us**. Healing means trusting that our integral behavior will bring us the partner we need. **I feel peace knowing my behavior with a person is fine.**

Day 252

Permission

I can be with a person any time I want. It is always OK. No matter what, even if they are wrong for us and it hurts, we can always be with anyone if we need to. If a relationship is unfulfilling and we can't cut the cord, if we want that charmer so much it makes us want to cry, if an individual feeds every obsessive impulse we have, all behavior with other people is allowed. Permission is so healing. As we become our own authority, we give ourselves permission to do what we need to do around potential partners. We ask ourselves how this person feels to us. If we feel bad in being around a person, then we use our feelings to get clarity about our motives. We ask why we want to feel bad. Is the pain easier to take if we think it is coming from outside of ourselves? On this journey, we don't need to hurt ourselves unnecessarily; however, today we give ourselves permission if we are compelled to be with any person. Letting ourselves go through the experience with the knowledge that we have the skills to take care of ourselves, no matter what the outcome, builds self-trust. The gift of permission is that sooner or later we will want to be with people who treat us well, and we will no longer need to hurt ourselves around partnership. **I trust in my ability to take care of myself in any way that I need to.**

Day 253

Emotional Armor

I take off my emotional armor around safe people. We often approach love as a battle. We have elaborate protections to defend us from being hurt. Even though our emotional armor may protect us from getting injured, sooner or later that protection is more painful than the pain we want to avoid. Now we notice that our armor deflects not only pain, but also joy. Today, we gently take off the heavy emotional armor we have worn for a lifetime. Now we know we are not at war with a partner. When we let go of our defense mechanisms, we lightly take the steps of intimacy one at a time. Each moment that we progress in our healing, we build faith gently and firmly in our ability to determine who is safe. Each piece of emotional armor we drop helps us to let in a wonderful partner. **I determine who I can trust. Then when I feel safe with someone, I peel off my emotional armor.**

Day 254

Letting Go

I let my partner deal with perplexing or troubling situations. When our partner has a burning issue pop up in life, we can usually see many ways that the situation could be handled. Objectivity gives us great abilities to problem-solve for people; we are detached from the issue. Usually, though, it is best to keep our hands off of another person's problems unless we are specifically asked for help or advice. The journey to healing means that we release the relentless desire to control other people. Now we give people the unspoken trust in their capabilities when we respect their choices. Obviously balance is important, and often others do need help, but letting a person deal with their own life sends the message that we have confidence in their ability to handle difficult situations. It also means we have our own lives to attend to. **I keep my hands off of my partner's difficulties unless asked for my help.**

Day 255

Simplicity

I keep things simple with potential partners. Being stuck means that we reject simplicity. We are usually trapped inside of our issues whenever we find ourselves mulling over a problem or trying to force a solution. For example, one woman's husband had not bought her flowers in three months. She was concerned about what this meant. She was also trying to hint that she wanted flowers. Then she realized that simplicity is the antidote; she told the plain, honest truth. When she took the risk to tell him she wanted flowers, he was delighted to buy them. Now he knows a good way to please her. She also realized that if he could not or would not meet her needs, she could buy herself flowers! Like her, to heal around partnership, we simplify life by doing the next right thing in front of us. Simplicity is straightforward. Keeping our relationships with other people easy to understand and easy to deal with, we have a greater chance of happiness and harmony. Often many things work out well in relationships without our direct intervention. Today we know that the temptation to overwhelm ourselves by inviting complications into our partnership is outdated. We firmly let go of all complications. **I keep things simple in my relationships. I let go of what I cannot control.**

Day 256

Using People

I abstain from using others. When we are stuck, we fear that there will never be enough for us. We assume that we need to manipulate, control, and use people in order to get what we need. Many of us don't realize that giving means to confer without expectation of reward, while receiving is taking something that is offered to us. If we are using other people on a conscious, or even subconscious, level to selfishly meet our own needs, we are not givers; we are not even truly receivers because we are not accepting what is offered. Instead we are manipulating to get what we need. Using another also doesn't feel good because a natural fear is built into the action; when we use someone else we assume that they will attempt to use us in return. Now we know we do not need to use another person; we know that we have enough resources of our own, and that we even have a surplus to give away. As we progress, we give freely and then accept in return. **I freely give to people.**

Day 257

Letting Go

I let go.

"Letting go is not dropping the rope that connects us to safety. It is opening our hands to the gifts our Higher Power is waiting to bestow on us."—Jack T.

Letting go is the only way to resolve our partnership issues. Letting go sounds so simple, yet it takes great courage. We want the person to be there on our timetable and they're not, we fear getting older and still "The One" doesn't appear, or we hold on in desperation to an individual who can't give us what we need because sometimes even an unavailable person seems better than being with no one. Even though it is challenging, letting go means that "just for today" we walk the path of healing. That means surrendering our efforts at controlling another person, ourselves, or the outcome of a relationship. As we walk this road we know that letting go is possible. **I open myself to the age old solution of letting go all through this day.**

Day 258

Old Behaviors

I release seduction, control, guilt, and manipulation to hook or hold onto a partner. Women are taught how to entrap a partner by the media, by romance novels, and by national women's magazines. Many powerful influences sell us a bag of tricks to "catch" a partner; however, womanhood is not a magic act. True availability on the emotional level is about being ourselves without relying on tricks to "catch" a person. Being stuck in our partnership issues is about pretense and control. Today we know we don't need to pull tricks out of a bag. Old behaviors used to entice or trap an individual may work, yet the price for us is dangerously high. Today we bravely release all old behaviors as we let in an emotionally available partner. **Today I know that who I am is good enough. I release old behaviors.**

Day 259

Outcomes

I let go of outcomes. Our society is outcome-oriented. We generally pride ourselves on what we can accomplish. The goal is often valued more highly than the process. Those of us healing our relationship issues can get "stopped dead in our tracks" by focusing on the outcome we want from this work. Whether we see marriage, partnership, or having children as the goal of our journey, we can be literally immobilized when we do not reach our goal as we expect to. The process of healing is miraculous, yet many times it does not look the way we think it will; it does not work on set timetables.

If we find that we are not achieving the outcomes we set for ourselves, it is important to honor all the progress we have made. Today we do not get tripped up, or despondent. An open heart, a freedom from self-hatred, the manifestation of our dreams, and joy are all benefits of healing. We trust that our blessings will lead us to the situation that is right for us when the time is right. Transformations will take place. The outcomes we want will manifest when we do this work; but now we accept that the timing and the general external appearance may look different than we anticipate. **I enjoy the freedom of letting myself be who I am. I worry less about outcomes.**

Day 260

Truth

I speak the truth to potential partners. Many of us learned to hide the truth, to protect other people's feelings, and to deny the reality of situations. Even though we fabricated and denied our truth, our relationships still never seemed to work out as we had hoped. Today we stop the cycle by speaking our truth and by letting a person face the reality of the situation. We know that when we speak the truth, we save everyone hardship and pain in the long run. If we are angry, we say so. If we feel joyful, we tell our partner the truth. Although truth telling takes practice and courage, we are worth all the discomfort this may cause in us and around us. Now we know that honesty sets us free. We are worth the investment of truth-telling in our relationships with our partners. Today we tell the truth to set ourselves free. **I have the courage to identify the truth and speak it out loud to my partner.**

Day 261

Surrender

I release the need for struggle and suffering.

"Surrender means to move to the winning side."—Anonymous

Love is comfortable, warm, and tender; however, we are often used to struggle and suffering in relationships. We are unaccustomed to having true love in our partnerships. All relationships have conflict and problems; however, an imbalance of joy vs. suffering can signal a lack of love. Today when we notice ourselves consistently struggling and suffering in a partnership, this may be a good indicator that love is not present in the relationship, or that some serious miscommunication is occurring. In this case, we put up the white flag of surrender around struggle and suffering. We are too wise to stay stuck in pain any longer. Now we look for a better way. Love isn't dramatic. We know that drama is comfortable only because we have practiced it for so long. Today, with joy, we reclaim our right to a love relationship that works. **I release the need for upset in my relationship.**

Day 262

Getting Out of Ourselves

I get out of myself for fun.

"Isn't it boring thinking about yourself all the time?"—Michelle

We have much to share with other people, but we are sometimes incapable of loving an emotionally available partner when we are stuck. This healing process is about getting out of ourselves and out of the obsessive focus with what is going on in our lives. We were meant to explore the richness of life through sharing our experiences. Asking others how they are doing helps us so much; it is amazing how such a simple gesture can connect us to others. When we reach out we learn about others, too. Healing means being emotionally available—so this is a great day to try it! Today if we find ourselves stuck in our own dilemmas, we know that our partnership issues have kicked up and that it is time to get out of ourselves. **Today I get out of myself and am of help to someone else.**

Day 263

Fault-Finding

I abstain from blaming my partner. If we are involved with people who consistently hurt us, then we need to take responsibility for the individuals that we are choosing. Our partners are not responsible for our life challenges. While it is true that often a person can complicate our lives for various circumstantial reasons, such as having to travel out of town for a period of time or having challenging family members, our fault-finding will not help the situation. Even if they are acting inappropriately, blaming them won't have the desired effect. If we feel the need to point out someone's shortcomings to them, chances are that our own issues are popping up. Any urge to find fault with other people signals that we are having an uncomfortable feeling or that we are in an uncomfortable situation. If someone is not right for us, the urge to blame may be signaling we need to release them. If the urge to find fault feels insincere, we may be trying to deflect love from an available person. By taking responsibility for our part in the situation and moving into our feelings when we feel the desire to nitpick someone, we are empowering ourselves. No matter what the message of our fault-finding, only by examining our own part in the relationship do we mend the issue. Today we release blame because it does not feel good to us, it upsets the person we love, it wastes our energy, and it diverts us from where true healing happens—within us. **If I notice a desire to find fault with my partner or people in general, I know my partnership issues are rising up.**

Day 264

Legalization

I legalize all potential partners. When we hear the suggestion to try legalizing all people, we may wonder, "What if I go crazy and am with even more inappropriate people? What if I get hurt? What if I don't like anyone and am alone forever? What if I act out? What if? What if?" Today let's surrender our fears and give this radical idea a try. We have been told since we were little girls who is legal and acceptable, and who is not. We learned from various influences: our parents, religions, and the media. But this is our chance to figure out who works best for **us** in partnership. The process of legalizing potential partners is where self-trust is born and nurtured. Today we legalize **all** people, and we do that as we are comfortable. Some of us can dive in and date all types of people now, while some of us may feel more comfortable legalizing one type of person at a time. Whatever way we choose to legalize potential life-mates, the only question to ask as we experience a person is, "How does this individual feel to me?" This is the exploration part of the healing process. All people are legal and of equal value: older, younger, tall, short, rich, poor, thin, heavy, available, and unavailable. Today we know that all potential partners are legal; we determine which types of people are good for **us. Today I decide all people are legal.**

Day 265

Passive-Aggression

I notice when I am passive-aggressive. Passive aggressive behavior manifests as never being willing to give the other person what they want, being consistently late, procrastinating, treating people disrespectfully, controlling, fearing competition, feeling victimized, lying or making excuses, and quietly making it known that something is wrong. Noticing when we are being passive-aggressive is the first step to changing this behavior. Then we need to let go of all passive-aggressive behavior. Although this is a tall order, it is possible. Noticing when we are acting passive-aggressively is the first step, which leads to acceptance, and then to releasing it. Now we know that in order to heal our relationship issues, we appropriately express our needs. We show up for our partner consistently, honestly, and on time. **Today I let go of my need to be passive-aggressive.**

Day 266

Behavior with Potential Partners

I love my behavior with people. As we journey through the process of healing, it may be difficult to accept our behavior with potential partners. It is always appropriate to increase our repertoire of behaviors with people, but the most important thing is to love who we are. Who we are is just fine. When I was healing, I met a man at a party who told me he was traveling to Europe for six months following his graduation. Then he wanted to move out of state. I chose to date him anyway, and was hurt when he followed through on his plans! From this I learned that our behavior often says clearly what we cannot say out loud. My behavior was talking. I wanted a relationship; however, I was still scared of getting close. He was a great choice, because I didn't have to risk real intimacy. He was leaving. When I realized what was really going on, I just noticed my behavior instead of judging myself. Then we ended the relationship. Soon after, I met and fell in love with my husband.

Now as we heal, we realize that trusting our behavior as it is in the moment is always the best option. Whether we question ourselves, wish we were like other women, or try to control ourselves, everything we do is OK. We are exactly where we need to be in the process of healing. We know that our unique behavior will lead us to the partner who is right for us when the time is right. **Today I respect every part of my behavior around people.**

Day 267

Being Who I Am

I let myself be who I am around potential partners. We often attempt to follow someone else's rules about how we "should" behave in order to get what we wants from a partner; however, today we are our own authority on what works for us in relationships. Many of us have elaborate ideas of what we should do around partnership. We have incorporated a huge body of "wisdom" from various sources. By this time, we act almost exclusively as we think we "should," rather than in ways that are comfortable and natural for us. Today is the day to give this internal dating guru her notice! The only way to heal our issues is to let go of behaviors that have kept us from being real with another person. Who we are is wonderful; pretense is not necessary to attract the person who can meet us beautifully. Being authentic may feel a bit strange at first. We may not be attracting as much attention as before; but those who appreciated all of our externalized feminine wiles never got to know us. Today even if the number of potential partners we attract is less, the quality of the individuals will be better. Our match will present themselves. **I honor quality rather than quantity. I am myself around other people.**

Day 268

Role Playing

I abstain from playing a role in a relationship. In our society, women are encouraged to develop the trait of playacting in relationships. We are taught that we should never show our true self to another person. Leading women's magazines bombard us with tips and trademarks of womanly behavior that will help us "nab" and keep a partner. What ends up happening, though, is that neither person is ultimately satisfied in the end. One day we begin to shed our false masks; then our partners are surprised because the women they thought they were with are in actuality very different. Today we are aware enough to identify the stifling function of role-playing. We see that being who we are is good enough. Although releasing cultural indoctrination is hard and takes great courage, the pay-offs yield great dividends. Walking through all of our fears, today we proudly bring ourselves to a relationship. **I take off all masks, and I let go of the safety of a role.**

Day 269

Teasing

I abstain from teasing people. Teasing signals we have no intention to go further with a potential partner. We want to hold all of their attention to us. We make them a hostage. Engaging in the behavior of teasing is always OK, yet we need to be clear that teasing is a function of our partnership issues. Provoking an individual with no intention of following through is a technique used to gain power over someone else; we get our needs met while in the end pushing a person away. Teasing others usually results in their frustration; however, teasing also hurts us because we are not giving ourselves the chance to be truly intimate with someone. If teasing is part of our relationship challenges, we become aware of the behavior, get help, and then let go of it.

If I notice I am teasing a potential partner, I let go of the behavior.

Day 270

Stop Signal

I slow down and go inside my soul to feel my natural stop signal with a partner. Now we trust that our desires for fulfillment with a partner will ebb and flow. Healing returns us to that very assured place within ourselves that doesn't hold on to a person for fear that we will never be able to love them again. We know that there will always be fresh new love experiences for us to participate in. In the past, we rarely had any idea when we wanted to stop with an individual or even how to stop. We may have stopped loving a person long before we were satisfied. Our reasons for doing this included being afraid to give our love to them, or feeling that we had to follow some arbitrary societal dictate. Now we know that our partnership issues are about scarcity and lack. When we are stuck, we fear that if we take a breather we will never get to be with this person again. Today, although we cannot and should not ever try to control what another person does, to the extent that it is possible, we are our own authority. When we are fulfilled in love with another person, we take a breather from them with trust that new love experiences are just around the corner. **I honor my own internal pace. When I am fulfilled, I take a breather.**

Day 271

Actions

I trust every action I take. There is meaning to all of our actions, even actions that do not appear to make sense on the surface. All the things we do make sense, even if an action isn't "rational." If we are pushing away available people and can't understand why, we trust that our behavior makes perfect sense. If we are still seeking out unavailable individuals, our issue has a message for us. Intimacy may still seem too scary; we may still be afraid that we will get hurt. Trusting all our actions is important. Although we may not always like what we do, our actions give us concrete information about where we are on our journey. Our actions may not get us where we want to go in each and every situation, but the actions do make sense. We pay attention by stopping and checking in to see what's going on in our lives. Often if we are not acting "rationally," we may have too much going on in our lives to invite a partner in, we may still be grieving past relationships, or we may still be in too much fear. No matter what actions we are taking around partnership; let's remember that there is no judgment involved in the healing process. Only with information do we move on to acceptance of our progress and to profound change. **I trust all my actions, even the "irrational" ones.**

Day 272

Men

I abstain from control around men. Men don't usually regulate their behavior around women. Most men do feel pressure to have a good job, a cool car, and clean clothes; however, men generally allow themselves to be who they are with a woman to a much greater extent than most of us. Today we learn from male behavior and incorporate these wonderful aspects of men into our lives. As women, especially today, we are bombarded with cultural messages of how to behave around men. We feel pressure to earn our own money, to have a "perfect" body, to cook well, and to be pleasing toward a man at all times. We have forgotten that it is OK to be who we are with men. Showing the truth of ourselves to a man makes a powerful statement. Not every man will respond to us when we relinquish control of our behavior around them, but we only need one wonderful partner. Let's trust that there is a man out there waiting to see us in all our unique glory; we have exactly what he needs, and he wants to meet us. **Today I do not control myself or my behavior around a man.**

Day 273

The Goal

I examine my goal for healing today. When we begin the process of healing, we usually want clear answers as to when we will get to our self-conceived goal. Marriage or partnership is often our goal; however, we can inhibit our progress if we get focused on outcomes. Marriage may take some time to materialize for some of us, or as we move along the path we may decide that marriage is not the way for us to reach our potential in this lifetime. Whatever result emerges, the important thing to keep in mind is that the **road** to resolving our partnership issues is to be respected. Usually we do not see a cultural mirror of our journey; this makes trusting the process very challenging. Today, though, we know that where we are is exactly right. We see that the goal is not as important as the journey. Our society is primarily goal-oriented, but healing is not linear; it is holistic. One day at a time, we surrender any future goal and focus on where we are right now. **I decide that my process is more important than my goal.**

Day 274

Keeping Up with the Jones's

I abstain from trying to keep up appearances. Women sometimes take abuse, neglect, or criticism from partners and try to keep up appearances so that other people will think we are in a successful relationship. The focus on what other people think gets us into a lot of trouble. Many of us have experienced much pain from being with people who seemed to have it all: looks, money, and possessions. Behind the externals, though, and in the center of the relationship, the appearances may have contrasted with reality. Now if some people in our lives are not pleased with our choice of a partner or make snide comments because the individual doesn't fit traditional notions of the "right" person, we let the comments go or set boundaries where appropriate. Today we are our own authority; we make good choices in partners. Now we look beyond the façade, release the obsession with appearance, and choose an emotionally available partner. **What others think of me is none of my business. I "let the chips fall where they may."**

Chapter Summary: Letting go of control is the most advanced level of emotional maturity that you have attempted so far; however, you are getting a sense of freedom every time you release your will. At this point, you may be enjoying feelings of relief that you do not have to play any more games. You are learning that trying to change yourself to connect with a partner is destructive and self-defeating.

Right now, identify 3 ways you are letting go of control. Notice 2 times this month that you stopped yourself from using people to get what you want. Look at 1 way you see your behavior differently. Are you letting yourself be who you are to a greater extent? Do you notice now when you have the urge to hide in relationships? Be glad about all your progress. Remember you are letting go of the control you have held onto for a lifetime. If you experience some bumps in the road, this is normal. The process of growing up on an emotional level is challenging.

One bump that may occur is that you may be attracting a smaller amount of people than you did before you started this process. Although this is confusing and scary, be aware that this result is common for women on this path. Do not fear. This simply means that as you are shedding your false masks, you are attracting people who can more adequately fulfill you. They may come in smaller quantities; just remember that you only need one emotionally available partner. That person is patiently waiting to meet **you**.

Now that you have let go of control and are open on a deeper level, you are ready to experience the true freedom of your spiritual self. The next chapter outlines the healing that love and spirituality bring to your partnership. Get ready to see how sharing your whole self with a partner lets love in.

Phase III Summary: In **Phase III** you completed the most difficult part of this journey. You learned to handle and process challenging situations and feelings. You learned how to release control of yourself and others. You also learned how to honor your true self. Now you are very skilled at taking care of yourself emotionally. At this point, you are emotionally mature.

Phase IV will complete your journey to share love with an emotionally available partner. In this last phase, you will learn how to connect with your own spiritual self, how to love another person more fully, and how to celebrate your process. I have also put a chapter on relationships and commitment at the end of **Phase IV** to offer you support as you maintain an emotionally available partnership; however, finding the relationship that is right for you may happen at any time on the journey. You may already be sharing love with an available person, you may not meet someone until after the year is up, or you may decide that partnership is not your focus now after all. Wherever you are is just fine. I put the relationship chapter at the end of the book so that you do not get attached to partnership as the goal.

The true goal of this healing process is to love and accept every part of yourself—physical, mental, emotional, and spiritual. When you love every part of yourself, you experience real power and freedom. Then you are ready to love an emotionally available partner. Enjoy every minute of your release. You deserve it.

Phase IV

♥♥♥♥

Power and Freedom

·10·

Love and Spirituality

Chapter 10 will show you the connection between love and spirituality. Ranging from acceptance and abundance to faith and miracles, this chapter will remind you of the immense healing power of your spirit. You will learn how to listen to the voice of your soul as you interact with potential partners, how to rely on a power greater than yourself to bring an emotionally available partner into your life, and how to honor your own divinity. Enjoy this chapter because you are a miracle. You deserve a wonderful relationship!

Day 275

Spirituality

I let my Higher Power meet my needs. Many of us have been running on our "own steam" for a very long time in relationships. We have been trying to make relationships happen. We believe in our own power to steer the course of the relationship, or we may abdicate our power and give it to the person in our lives. Whatever the case, we have forgotten that a power greater than any human being, man or woman, exists in the universe. To heal our partnership issues, we now acknowledge that human power is not the sole resource for us. Today we tune into the power of the universe. A loving power that cares about us can be conceived differently by everyone. Some of us see this power as the ocean, the wind, nature, Great Spirit, or a group of people. Whatever way we imagine it, it is there patiently waiting for us to ask for help. Whenever we let go even a little, a Higher Power is waiting to satisfy all our needs. What makes believing in a Higher Power challenging is that the answers may not come as we think they should or on our timetable; we may wonder if a Higher Power even hears us. Today, though, we trust that we are heard. We know that whenever we give up control even a little bit, grace happens. **Today I let my spirituality guide me, as well as asking for human aid.**

Support

I am supported by a Higher Power.

"I went to the beach and tried to stop the waves from breaking, but it didn't work."—Don

Realizing we are only a part of the whole is challenging for all people. For those of us who choose unavailable partners, though, the humility of asking for help from a Higher Source is hard. We have been running on self-will for a long time. Although human power is finite, the idea of surrendering all of our plans, manipulations, desires, hopes, and dreams to some ephemeral concept can be terrifying. The magic, though, is that letting a Higher Power into our lives allows us to relax and trust. Most of us have not experienced much relaxation and trust with people or in our relationships; therefore surrendering to the support of a loving power greater than ourselves gives us a new experience in love. Whether our Higher Power is the ocean, nature, God, Goddess, or a doorknob, we are lightening our process when we give up control. As long as we see a loving creative force outside of us who wants all our good to occur as more powerful than we are, then we tune into all the support available to us from the universe. **Today I let go. I let a Higher Power carry me as I heal my partnership issues.**

Release

I release control to the care of a Higher Power. It is fun to let go. Willful control takes a lot of work and doesn't allow much room to play. A Higher Power is a force that is greater than us. It is more powerful than any human being. We may have trouble releasing control to a Higher Power as we heal our partnership issues, however. We may wonder if some ephemeral being even cares about us. When we want that right relationship to present itself to us and it doesn't; when we want our partner to appear right now and it takes more time than we think it should for them to manifest; or when we try to practice honesty with other people and experience many obstacles, the tendency to get impatient is natural. If we try to get in there to "help" control outcomes, though, we may slip backward. Trusting in something larger and more powerful than us can soothe us in moments when we want to "direct the show." It is always appropriate for us to care for ourselves and do the necessary footwork to interact with people, practice intimacy, and manifest our dreams; however, letting go to a Higher Power feels good and relieves us of pressure. When we know that there is something bigger than us managing our lives well, we are comforted. Then we use our precious time on this planet to play. **Today I let go of control for fun.**

Day 278

Rescue

I let my Higher Power save me.

"Sooner or later, humans will always let us down."—Anonymous

We don't want to believe that there isn't someone who can be all things to us all the time. The fairy tales promise this. The rescuer always arrives at just the right time to save the princess who, without the intervention, would be doomed. In real life, though, no one can save us except ourselves. Even when we do all we can to rescue ourselves, sometimes we cannot measure up to that fairy tale personage either. That is why so many women become hopeless of ever finding the right mate, because our human power is limited. Learning to trust and rely on the spiritual power of the universe gives us a true rescue. It is not the job of any other person on the planet to rescue us, especially not the job of our partner. We have options today to heal our partnership issues, including utilizing resources to get the help we need, trusting our own power, and ultimately relying on a power that is greater than ourselves. **Today I rely on the spiritual power of the universe to perform a true rescue for me.**

Day 279

Divine

I am a divine being right now. Our divinity is part of being human. Part of choosing an emotionally available partner is the honoring of our own extreme goodness. Our partnership issues are about the fear that we are not good enough for a loving relationship. We fear that we can't make a relationship work. The relationship we need most is with our own spirit, though. Fortunately that relationship is always available to us. Finding the spiritual part of ourselves is essential to healing, for it is impossible for us to either abuse ourselves or allow others to abuse us once we see our own magnificence. The Buddha said that anyone born as a human being is already highly evolved spiritually; it is a tremendous accomplishment for all of us to just be here in human form. Today let's remember that who we are right now is precious and divine; we are each a sacred treasure. **For the next 24 hours I explore my own sacredness.**

Day 280

New/Old Way of Loving

I learn my new/old way of loving. We are children of a Higher Power. We were brought into this world as beings of pure love. We don't actually need to fight to attain a loving nature; in fact we were born with it. Now we backtrack as far as we need to in order to uncover that pure part of us. Our new/old way of loving is new because we are rediscovering it by letting go of old behaviors that no longer serve us, and old because we have always had it buried underneath the tangle of love patterns we developed in order to survive. Today we affirm that we enjoy following our spirit's directions in love relationships. Now we know that our new/old way of loving is leading us to a wonderful, available relationship. **I uncover the treasure of my new/old way of loving.**

Day 281

Pacing

I love my spirit's own pace. Healing is reclaiming who we are and our unique pace in relationships. Our pace does not need to look like anyone else's. It is futile to compare ourselves just because we aren't moving as fast or as slow as someone else. Today let's really see how fast we want to go with a person and at what pace we feel comfortable. Our own pace for moving into a relationship is something special to discover. The process of illuminating our own love pace is not about rules. We become our own authority. We don't follow specific instructions from a book or magazine telling us how to hook or hold on to a potential partner; instead, we respect our own pace with a person. **In this moment, I cherish my own pace in relationships.**

Day 282

Miracles

I know a miracle is just around the corner.

"Don't give up before the miracle."—Anonymous

We will experience good relationships. The miracle will happen. All the challenges, struggle, pain, and slogging through will bring us to where we want to go. It is easy to get hopeless and fed up as we move through this process, though. Fearlessly facing ourselves on this path takes courage. Confronting the reasons we have been in unfulfilling relationships with unavailable people, or have been unable to sustain working partnerships, is hard. No matter what our experience in healing, the miracle is waiting right around the corner for us. We will receive the healing of our partnership issues that we crave; therefore, today we do not give up before the miracle. **For this day only, I am willing to receive miracles.**

Day 283

Total Peace

I make total peace with potential partners. People deserve to be treated peaceably. Our culture has portrayed problematic partners as the enemy of women; however, we are not at war with those we partner. Other people have no power over us, unless we allow it. Many of us have experienced partners who were neglectful or abusive. We may feel jaded or hurt. Today, though, we realize that **our** old ideas keep us in bondage. Re-conceptualizing our relationship with potential partners heals us. When we make peace with other people we see the wonderful features of safe, available, and appropriate individuals all around us. Our problematic past experiences do not need to be repeated, but we do need to make peace with other people in order to sidestep these problems. Making peace does not mean that we stick around individuals who are unsafe for us or that we always love every person's behavior. What peace with others means is accepting people unconditionally, with all of their foibles and fantastic features. People are good, kind, and gentle. The sooner we believe this, the sooner those individuals manifest in our lives. **Today I accept others. I know that my peaceful relationship with people manifests in those I meet.**

Divinity

I awaken to my own divinity. When we are stuck, we balk at the idea that we are divine beings. We feel unworthy of love, are afraid we can't love, or are fearful of potential partners. We forget that our birthright is to love, that we are divine beings created to love divinely, and that a wonderful life-mate is waiting for each of us. The process of resolving our partnership issues is about uncovering that natural lover within us so that we can love ourselves body, mind, and soul. Then we attract someone who respects our sacredness. Healing means that we understand that love between partners is about sharing our divinity. By letting a person love us, and in turn loving them back and honoring their divinity, we spread love on the planet. **I know that love is my birthright.**

Day 285

Natural Love

I re-experience the natural lover inside myself. Reclaiming the natural lover buried within us means going back as far as we need to in our lives to remember our true love responses, or imagining them if we cannot remember. Babies and two year olds who haven't had their natural love bred out of them yet show us how natural love works. Children respond to people with curiosity, a lack of fear, and the expectance of love and care. Interacting with potential partners can be just as simple if we let go of our programming. Of course, we do not want to let go of the common sense that comes with age and experience; however, we can return that small precious child within us all who knows how to love in a healthy way. Returning to the natural lover within us is an experience of uncovering the basis of who we are—beings of pure love. Though the process may take time and patience, it heals. **Today I love naturally.**

Day 286

The Spiritual Feature of Men

I see the spiritual feature of men. Men are miraculous creatures who have many wonderful qualities. They are admirable, adorable, and precious. Men are often good at setting boundaries for themselves, know that they are entitled to pleasure, can really listen to women, and are good at noticing our amazing qualities. For all their villainization in America's current pop-culture, men have the ability to truly love. There are wonderful fathers, brothers, workers, and partners out there. Not every man is right for us, yet today we have the chance to meet men who are wonderful. Letting positive male energy into our lives is so much fun, too. Today nothing has to be so serious. Men are children of the universe; they are not as different from us as we may think. Men want to be happy and loved, too. The more nurtured men feel, the better able they are to let us shine. **For the next 24 hours, I honor men.**

Day 287

Attunement

I tune into my partner and my soul as I love. Love feels good. For those of us who have chosen unavailable partners in the past, though, love experiences can bring up major issues. Being present and in tune with our partner may seem impossible at times; therefore, the moments when we earnestly need to put our healing into play are during love experiences. Also, in those moments of love, we must remember that we do not have to do this alone. We have another person in front of us with their own issues and needs surfacing, too. Sharing intimately with our partner by gently asking them how they are feeling, what they need, and what they want helps. Then taking the further risk of sharing our needs, desires, and feelings attunes us to a person as well. Love is risky, yet it is worth it. Love is about warmth and caring. Now we know that tuning in to our partner feels good, because attunement brings harmony. **Today I am attuned to my needs and the needs of my partner.**

Day 288

Gratitude

I express my thankfulness. Even though the energy of gratitude builds on itself, it is challenging for many of us to feel grateful when we are not in a relationship. Even if we have a person in our lives, gratitude can be hard to come by. We have many wonders in our lives to be thankful for today, though. Now we know that focusing on our gratitude reaps real rewards. As we write three things we are grateful for, we see that we are blessed beyond measure. For starters, we have loved ones, our own self-love, nature, the next twenty-four hours, and the knowledge that we have progressed far on our journey to heal. No matter what shape our gratitude takes, today we remember what we are truly thankful for and let the light in. **I am grateful for the joys in my life.**

In This Moment

In this moment, I am perfect, complete and loved. This moment is perfect. We have been moving toward this moment for our whole lives. Everything we have done has led us here. Let's take some time today to really appreciate the moment. Listening to the sound of the birds singing, seeing the light streaming in through the window, touching the softness of our own skin, we know that right now we are just fine. The experience is right. Complete, cared for, and healing, we know that this moment was created for us to enjoy. With a deep breath, we relax and enjoy this moment. **Today I appreciate the moment.**

My Soul

I let my soul tell me who I am interested in. Inside ourselves is a still, peaceful place that knows who we are interested in. Separating the ego from the soul is difficult, yet it is possible. Many of us are very invested in partnering who we "should" be with. We were raised to know what types of people were "marriage material," and what types weren't. Now we see that whenever we are trying to manufacture an attraction that is weak or even nonexistent, we are stuck in our issues. Women often think that if a person is interested us, we "should" feel the same. We try to talk ourselves into feeling interest in people we may not even truly like, people whose values are very different than ours. We may go to the other extreme, too, by talking ourselves out of a strong attraction we do feel because they are not the "right" type for us. Whenever our issues rise up, connecting with that soulful place inside gives us all the information we need about who interests us. Now we know our partnership issues are not out to hurt us when they pop up; our issues are only trying to get our attention so that we can love an emotionally available partner. **I release all "shoulds" that dictate my attractions. I let my soul direct me.**

Day 291

Faith

I have faith. For women, loneliness is hard to deal with. Even though many of us choose on some level not to be in a relationship, the loneliness is terrible. We experience the challenge of trusting that we will be taken care of around sex, love, and partnerships. Whenever we begin to doubt and fret about when or how it will happen for us, our hopelessness signals that our partnership issues are rising up.

Our fears are a signal to move deeper inside. Now we ask questions. "Are we in an uncomfortable situation? Are we having an uncomfortable feeling? What is going on in our lives right now? If we weren't worried about our partnership status, what else would we be concerned about?" Learning to honor our lack of faith as an indication that we need to take care of ourselves helps us. Our relationship issues are not surfacing to hurt us; the issues only pop up to get our attention. Actually our issues are trying to move us toward healing. Today we have faith that we will come out the other side. **I have faith in my own power to heal.**

Day 292

Loving Myself

I love myself. Life can be tough for everyone on the planet. That's why love is so important for all of us. Our issues drive love underground, though. Therefore our process is essential for healing not only ourselves, but for restoring the world. We women who love ourselves unconditionally possess a greater ability to love our partners. Although we often have tangled relationships with ourselves and with partnership, today we make a decision to spread love on the planet. Emotional availability is about deep, profound love. Now we know that the work we are doing is promoting our healing and the healing of the world. **Today I glory in all of myself!**

Contribution

I share my experiences. Keeping a potential partner at arms length is a real symptom of our partnership issues. In the past, people were either bombarded by our experiences or completely left out of the loop because we have had difficulty sharing with them. Now we practice letting someone into our lives one day at a time. We have value. We have something to share with other people, whether it is the person in our life, another woman in the process of healing her partnership issues, or a child who can benefit by our experience. Our contributions help. Now we know that emotional availability is about sharing our experiences and giving to life. **I contribute to life.**

Day 294

An Open Heart

I open my heart to myself and to others. For many of us, heartbreaks happened early in our lives. From then on it seemed safer and more appropriate to keep our hearts closed. The heart, however, is an emotional center that needs to be open in order to function appropriately. Now we are learning that when we open our hearts to ourselves, we are also able to open our hearts to others. Maintaining an open heart takes practice. One exercise is to imagine a person in front of us and breathe warm, loving flames around them when we breathe in. As we breathe out, fan these loving, warm flames. This exercise works. It opens our hearts. The more we open our hearts to ourselves and to potential partners, even in the form of a meditation like this, the more clearly that we see that there are many people around us with whom we are able to be openhearted. Then we are better at knowing who to open our heart to. Try it—it really works. **I open my heart to safe people.**

Day 295

Natural Born Lovers

I am a natural born lover.

"Two year olds are like Buddhist sages. They aren't Buddhist sages, but they act in accordance with their inner natures."—Ron Epstein

We are all natural born partners. Little children have no fear of loving who they want, as they want, when they want to. When we are born, we come into this world as a being of pure love. We are the result of the ultimate creative act—the generation of new life. As we grew up, this natural knowledge of love may have been bred out of us; however, if we learned ineffective love behaviors, we can unlearn them. We learned how to love from our parents, the media, and from other models. While many of the love behaviors we learned are wonderful and work in our lives, other types of behaviors that we connect with love are dysfunctional. Today we let go of all outmoded behaviors we associate with love. Now we see that behind all that information, we know how to partner naturally. **I return to the natural lover inside of me.**

Day 296

The Right Person

I am becoming the right person.

"The light you seek is your own lantern."—The Buddha

Finding a partner is the great myth of fulfillment in our culture. Women are often waiting for another person to illuminate us, yet we do not need to wait! We all can share our knowledge and talents with the world in this moment, partner or no partner. In our world, it is easy to get distracted from our power. We may think, "I need someone to take care of me." "I need protection," or "I will be complete when I find that someone special." But thinking this way detours us from using and cultivating our precious and special gifts right now. Just for today, we know that we are in the process of becoming the right person because we are our own light. **I am not looking for the right person anymore because I nurture the right person in me.**

Day 297

Spirit

I touch base with my spiritual self and ask myself who I want. Our spirit is always unchanging. We can't lose it, sell it, or be completely alienated from our spirit. Many of us have lost touch with our spirit, though. Now our work is to reconnect with our spirituality. When we do touch base with our Self, we receive a magical gift. Our spirit knows who we truly need and want to be with. Whenever we are with someone and begin feeling joyful, calm, and good, our spirit is giving us information that we can grow with this person. The message is that they feed our soul. When we are generally discontented, angry, confused, upset, and depressed around a person, the voice of our spirit is sending a strong message. Today our task is to stay connected to this still voice. Now we honor what it is saying, even if that is difficult. Our spirit always gives us correct information; however, our minds are good at talking us out of what our spirit knows. Today let's practice tuning in and honoring our spirit. **Today I ask myself how this person affects my spirit.**

Day 298

Self-Definition

I define for myself what my spiritual life needs. We are worth all the time and commitment the process of healing takes. Many wonderful spiritual teachers are out there to help us; however, in the realm of spirituality some people want to help by giving advice where it is not needed. Many of us have accepted direction from others because we were unsure of ourselves; therefore, changing may be very challenging for us and for the people in our lives. If we have a friend, a religious institution, or parental influences trying to control our spiritual development, this is the appropriate time for us to set limits with them. We are on a spiritual path. Our process may look different than that of other people in our lives. It is important is to realize that, while people mean well, our journey belongs to us. Today we take the time to set boundaries with love where appropriate. Now we create our own definition of our spirituality. **I chart the course of my spiritual development.**

Day 299

Spiritual Acceptance

I accept my spirit just as it is in this moment.

"We are not human beings having a spiritual experience, but spiritual beings having a human experience."—Anonymous

We often have paid dearly from trying to "sell our soul" or attempting to somehow change who we truly are to be with a partner. Because there is nothing about us that needs to be changed on a spiritual level except to love and accept ourselves more, we have never been successful in trying to control ourselves, our partners, or situations for very long. Now as we heal our partnership issues, we may not be entirely happy with our behavior all the time, yet we trust that our essence is just fine. The desire to fit in and change ourselves can be oppressive in our world. Today we know that we do not have to dive into the cultural obsession. The person in our lives deserves to see all the radiance that we are—our spiritual being. Now we reveal ourselves when it is safe. **Today I know that my spirit is wonderful.**

Day 300

Abundance

4,800 potential partners are available right now in your area.

"There are lots of men in the city who want to have fun."—David Cheek

Even if we do not live in a city, there are many available people for us to partner with. We sometimes forget that there are others who want to connect with us as much as we want them. Our issues are about seriousness and scarcity. We believe that all the good people have already been taken; we fear that we will be left out. As a matter of fact, today there are more single people in the world than ever before. Scarcity is simply not realistic. We have the chance to pick with ease. There are many wonderful potential partners who would love to connect with us. Today is the day to remember that we are pulling from a field of plenty. All people are legal; it is always OK to interact with **anyone**. We need only determine who feels good to us. Then, shedding seriousness, we let ourselves play. Not every person will be good for us, yet we can trust that there are many loving individuals available for us right now. **Today I delight in the abundance of potential partners in my world.**

Day 301

My Soul

I trust my soul to lead me to an available partner who wants me. We have rarely let our souls lead us in interactions with partners; however, our souls know exactly who we need in a person. Acknowledging that a wealth of information exists inside of us detailing who works well for us is revolutionary. It can be hard to believe if we are used to listening to our fears, our parents, or the media. Underneath all the layers of rules and data we have been handed, however, our soul is patiently waiting for us to look inward for answers. By uncovering the layers of misinformation and misdirection we have been given and have given ourselves for so long, we are led to who we need to be with. Our souls want to direct us to a person who is non-abusive, kind, and available. Our task today is simply to tune into that trustworthy and wise part of ourselves that already knows exactly who we need. **I uncover the part of my soul that is directing me to a wonderful partner.**

Day 302

Plenty

There are plenty of people who are already just right for me.

"When you find yourself, you will see that there are 20 people in front of you who are just right for you."—Hillary Flye

Women who experience challenges in relating look for the flaw in a potential partner, the feature that makes it impossible for us to get close. Usually we do this to ourselves as well. Instead of focusing on the positives within ourselves, we pick ourselves mercilessly apart. We think, "I am too heavy. I don't have the 'right' clothes. I have a blemish on my chin." Today when we work to explore the richness and magic of who we are, we find ourselves; then we no longer judge on appearances. As we acknowledge our own magnificence, then we don't judge a book by its cover. When we meet someone; we see them. **In this moment, I see plenty of partners who are a good fit for me.**

Day 303

Authority

I let my spirit dictate who it wants, when it wants this person, and when it is full of love. Following our spirit's guidance yields better and happier love experiences for us. Listening to the voice of our spirit can be challenging, though. Our society does not often teach us to value the authority of our spiritual selves. We learn that if we aren't actively trying to "snag" a partner, or at least practicing time-tested feminine wiles, that we will never be OK. Listening to the voice of the soul informing us who we want, when we feel desire for them, and when we are satisfied, takes practice and courage. Because we may not have had much experience connecting with our spirit in this way, it can be helpful to run our discoveries by another safe person when we do get internal direction. That way we get a "reality check." Now we know that if we practice diligently and with the support of safe others, we will find tremendous rewards from following the dictates of our soul. **Today I delve into my spirit to discover who I want, how much of a person's company I want, and when I want them.**

Day 304

Abundant Choices

I let myself be abundant about all potential partners and then from within my soul choose who is right for me. Today there are actually more single people than ever in our society. We have an abundance of people to choose from. Too often, though, women are told about the shortage of available partners in our culture. This is terrorism on an emotional level. Today we do not buy into this belief. Now we try out anyone who appeals to our souls. We give ourselves the authority to choose the individual that is right for us. As we heal, we learn that there are many people out there; all types are legal. Then we begin to mingle, going within our souls during these interactions with potential partners. With practice, we get a sense of the type of person who works well for us. Today we explore the world about us and see the abundance of people who are just right for us. Then we let our soul dictate who we want. **I have an abundance of partners to choose from.**

Chapter Summary: Your spiritual self knows exactly who you need. Getting in touch with this gentle, subtle part of yourself takes practice; however, your core self is waiting patiently to help you choose an emotionally available partner. When you listen to your intuition, touch base with how you are feeling, and invite peace into your relationships, you are honoring your spiritual being.

Today take a few minutes to get quiet and centered. Listen inward to the voice of your spirit. Ask yourself questions. Ask, "What are my internal beliefs about the abundance of potential partners out there? Do I have faith that I will make it to the other side of my partnership issues? Do I believe I have a divine gift to share with the world? What do I want to share? Who do

I want to share it with?" When you have answered these questions, take some time to thank your spirit.

With practice you are getting better and better at identifying that still, quiet voice. Since connecting to your spiritual center is hard to do, it is imperative that you be gentle with yourself if you are not tuned in all at once. This is normal. As you continue on your journey, remember that you are a miracle. Every time you access the power and freedom of your spiritual being, you are moving closer to celebrating the journey. The next chapter will show you ways to congratulate yourself.

·11·

Celebrating Our
Journey

This chapter will help you to celebrate your process. You will become skilled at manifesting your dreams, at enjoying your newfound freedom and power, and at handling holidays and other events. This is the chapter that helps you toast to your success. Enjoy this large pat on the back. With every day that passes, you are closer to true love!

Day 305

Celebration

I celebrate who I am. We are miraculous creations of our Higher Power. Today is a day to celebrate. A wedding is traditionally regarded as a woman's day to have everything her way. Other than during nuptials, society offers women few opportunities to celebrate ourselves so formally and visibly; therefore, marriage takes on added significance for women. Some of us who have not married yet may feel excluded by society's traditions. If that is the case, today we can make a decision to celebrate ourselves. Celebrations feel good and affirm our lives. Joy, elegance, flowers, cake, special music, and good friends can make us feel special and appreciated. Whatever is going on in our lives right now is an occasion to celebrate; this day is important. Now we know that we have a unique place in the world. We are a reason to celebrate. **Today I celebrate myself.**

Day 306

Gratitude

I thank myself for giving myself love. When we are in love, we glow. People are charmed by our energy. Love lights us up from within. It is a profoundly wonderful experience when we give ourselves love, too. Love is a gift that radiates out from us. Gifts of love may seem like small acts, yet the world is healed each time we love. Gratitude for love's gifts also sets up its own energy that generates more love in the world. Love freely given to ourselves and to others creates a wonderful platform for healing; working out our partnership issues helps us all. For this reason, each time we practice love in our relationships with ourselves or with others, we truly thank ourselves for the wonderful gift we are giving. **I know that my gratitude is healing the planet.**

Day 307

Manifesting

I love to manifest my dreams. It is easy to lose track of our interests as we grow up. Society generally encourages its women to fit into neat categories and to put other people's interests above our own; however, today we reclaim our unique talents, dreams, and interests. What do we dream of? What are our goals and aspirations? What interested us as we grew up? Today we have the space in our lives to live our dreams. In fact, as soon as we let go of our obsessions with people, our challenging relationships, and all the drama, we find we have oodles of time on our hands. Being stuck in our partnership issues has drained us of much of our energy. Now that we have it back, we have a chance to rebuild our lives and do amazing things. **I live my dreams.**

Day 308

Adulthood

I am an adult woman around my attraction to a potential partner. Being an adult takes hard work and sometimes isn't fun. Too often in our culture women are labeled girls. We are told dependence is the easy route. We are encouraged to rely on other people's ideas of who we should partner with. It may be easier sometimes to depend on others, or to rebel against them; however, the price paid for this is too high. Today let's choose to be fully mature and claim our adult feminine power. Adulthood means honoring all of our attractions. We also honor those times that we do not feel attracted to a person or when we want to be alone. Female adulthood means owning our power and exulting in all our experiences of attraction. Today we are responsible for ourselves. **I have all my feelings for a potential partner,**

not just the ones society "allows" me as a woman.

Day 309

Personal Independence

I celebrate my personal independence. Autonomy represents a tremendous symbol to us. We are independent, even when we are in a relationship. We do need to be interdependent with a partner and with the world about us; however, many of us have gone to extremes and been codependent on our partners in our pasts. Interdependency means that we share our gifts, talents, resources and abilities with others, while we let them share with us. Codependency means that we use people almost like a drug or fix to distract us from our pain, our feelings, and our lives. Today we no longer need to hide behind another person through codependency. We are miraculous, strong, independent creatures. Being personally independent within a relationship gives us a greater grounding in our own strength. As we gradually become better able to share with a potential partner, rather than trying to see what we can get from them, we experience freedom. **I am personally independent.**

Day 310

Good Things

I honor my goodness. Choosing unavailable people means that we focus on our flaws, rather than on the many good things that we have to offer a partner; at a basic level, we don't feel good enough for an available partner. Today let's change our minds by taking some time to honor the good things in ourselves. Whether we are adorable, loving, fun, intelligent, affectionate, witty, or playful, have a gentle energy, a quick mind, are great dancers, or are adventurous, we now see that we each have special qualities that make us desirable to others. This is the time to explore what it is about us that is special. When we accept ourselves, our self-love helps us to see that an available person is waiting to love us. **I notice many good things in myself.**

Healing

I heal my heart.

"Healing is different than curing. It produces beautiful results."—Anonymous

Healing means that an ailment is brought to an end. When we are healed, we are free from a disorder. Curing suggests an antidote, a method, or a course of remedial treatment. While both healing and curing are necessary to address our partnership issues, and while a cure seems desirable, healing is a holistic approach to regaining our balance. Healing is hard and sometimes hurts, though. It is the longer route to freedom. In fact, when a wound is healing it sometimes itches, is painful, and takes a lot of focus. When we heal, we wonder when we will ever get better. We wish we could just take a pill or get a shot to figure this partnership stuff out; however, the healing process of life is miraculous in itself. Physical wounds do heal on our bodies. Our emotional wounds around partnership will heal too. As we heal, we learn that the real cure for us is not another person or a relationship. The only cure is to do the healing work and celebrate every step of the process. Although the results may look different than we think they should, and we may not experience healing on our timetables, the process does work. We are making our way to the other side! **Today I trust that my partnership issues are healing.**

Day 312

Life on Life's Terms

I trust in myself to live life on life's terms with potential partners.

"What contract did you sign?"—Marilyn

Many of us expect the fairy tale perfection of a relationship without being willing to do the work involved to sustain or nurture that partnership. Our culture promotes the "happily ever after" scenario. We don't usually see the background effort that contributes to a working partnership. If we saw behind other people's successful relationships, we would clearly see that both the partners work hard to maintain a healthy working relationship. Feeding love takes work. The pay off from learning to be right-sized and to love as a normal partner, in addition to a working relationship, is that we **get** to do the work every day. The work of a relationship itself is the gift. As we participate in actions that build, sustain, and constantly renew our love, we appreciate the discipline of showing up. We didn't sign a contract that said life would be easy around people and relationships; however, we are assured of great rewards from resolving our partnership issues. **I joyfully take action to contribute to a working partnership.**

Day 313

Pursuit

I pursue life passionately. Life is not about struggle; life is about pleasure. We may have had challenging and disheartening experiences in the past with partnership, but that time is over now. Today we assert our belief that life is about joy, not sorrow. If there are experiences we would like to try, we envision what it would be like to try these out. If there are potential partners that we want to connect with, we take positive steps to getting closer. If there are ways we would like to contribute, we offer our skills. We were put on this earth to enjoy ourselves. Today is the day to go after our dreams and aspirations with the sure knowledge that amazing things will happen to us. When we contribute to the universe even a little bit and explore all the richness available to us, we are pursuing life positively. **I pursue life with joy and happiness.**

Day 314

Freedom

I choose freedom. Journeying through this process gives us freedom from the obsession with potential partners, freedom from fear of others, freedom from the "shoulds" of our society, freedom from believing we did something to drive another person away, freedom from hurting ourselves, freedom from missing out on great available people, and freedom from self-hatred. Today we choose to be free. Freedom takes practice and hard work, yet freedom does occur as a result of walking this path. We are worth all the effort this healing process takes because our freedom will in turn free others. There are many examples of women who have healed their partnership issues. As we walk this path, we become lights to others on the journey too. **I know that**

freedom is my birthright.

Day 315

Adornment

I adorn myself to please myself and my partner. Our culture is obsessed with appearance. Women often feel less than if we are not perfect, immaculate, or at least in fashion. Being in balance, though, means a withdrawal from the competition. Healing means that we focus on what pleases us and what is pleasing to the individual we love. Re-conceptualizing appearance as a way to please another person allows us to be more moderate and giving. In our world, women have been taught to be one-sided around appearance. We may have learned that it is somehow wrong to want to please our partner with our appearance, that we need to please a person with our appearance in order to "hold them," or that we should only please ourselves. Whatever our past history around appearance; healing means that we adorn ourselves for mutual pleasure because it pleases us to make ourselves and a person we love happy. **I see appearance as a vehicle of love. I adorn myself for pleasure.**

Day 316

Beauty

I am beautiful inside and out. Adornment, flowers, the use of products to enhance our features, sensual fragrances, and wonderfully textured clothes can be pleasurable. For centuries many women have enjoyed a special interest in beauty. Today beauty may take a lot of our focus. Doing things to make ourselves beautiful feels good; it is only when our obsession with beauty as a way to entice, trap, or hold a partner takes over that we are in danger. Our culture bombards us daily with images of standardized feminine beauty. Those pictures don't tell the whole truth, though. For instance, while our models are lovely, most people agree that a woman who is skin and bones is not someone they want to hold at night when there is the opportunity to be with a soft, warm woman. As we heal our partnership issues, we know that beauty comes in many forms. Now we determine what beauty means to us. Our inner essence is as beautiful as our outer appearance; therefore, today we tend to our inner selves just as we tend to our physical beauty. **I embrace all**

of my beauty.

Day 317

Positive Changes

I have the ability to make positive changes. The great myth of "coupledom" promotes the idea that when we meet "The One," we can fulfill our dreams. Positive changes stem from inside, though, and changes can be very simple to enact. Today is the day to check in and ask questions. Ask, "What are my dreams and desires? Do I long to live in the country, to travel to distant lands, to explore new career options, to get a pet? What changes can I make today that would bring more positive energy into my life?" Reading this book is making a positive change in our day. Now we go even farther. Let's devote a few more minutes today to exploring positive changes we can implement in our lives for the next 24 hours, whether these are simple steps or elaborate visions of change. **I make positive changes in my life.**

Day 318

Success

I am a success. We are a success today, simply because we are healing. Now we know that each relationship that we have been in has brought us here where we have the courage to look our issues in the face. Our problems with partnership are not here to punish or immobilize us. In fact, the challenges recur powerfully until we learn the lessons that they have to teach us. Success means seeing the gifts that our past relationships have brought us. Success means noting all the gifts we have been given by the people in our lives. If challenges with a partner deepened our spirituality, if we learned what we don't want in a life-mate, if we received kindness or miracles, all our partnerships have taught us lessons. Today we know that all of the gifts that we have received ensure our healing. **I am a success because I see the gift of all my joy and pain with people.**

Day 319

Sex

I know that sex can heal me. Sex is powerful. It is wonderful, fantastic, charged, awesome, freeing, and healing. People in general have very complicated relationships to sex, and women in particular have been inundated with cultural messages about the significance of sex. All humans have sex, though. The purposes of sex are pleasure and to procreate if we choose to. Sexual energy can also be considered a divine gift made for communing with our Higher Power. For instance, the ancient Indian practice of Tantra, the grandfather of Hatha Yoga, considers the sexual union of partners as a practice which can lead to enlightenment for the couple. (See the Bibliography for resources.) No matter what sexual path we take, bottom line let's remember that sex is good and natural. Whatever methods of having sex, or not having it, that we want to engage in are fine as long as we are not hurting ourselves or someone else. **I celebrate my sexuality today.**

Day 320

Openness

I open to my partner. Being stuck in our partnership issues is about being closed off, frozen, and unwilling to stretch. Choosing an emotionally available partner asks us to open to people, to relationships, and to our feelings. So what does openness really mean? Openness suggests the ability to expand, unfold, and spread out. A truly open person is accessible and available. When we open to a safe, appropriate person, the process is beautiful. We learn to heal with someone else. We use the experience of the partnership to reach deeper into love. The challenge of unfolding before another person is the fear of being hurt or unloved; however, there is nothing to fear anymore. By healing we protect ourselves and love ourselves no matter what. Now we are so good at meeting our own needs, we know for certain that we are taken care of in all ways. Then we can take the risk of opening. **I open to my partner knowing that I am safe.**

Day 321

The Banquet Table

I eat from the banquet table. We don't have to take crumbs today. The wealth of potential partners in the world provides an elaborate smorgasbord of people for us to choose from. Despite fearful assertions from various "authorities" and "experts" that there are not enough good people out there, today we know that many stellar individuals are available. We know that they want a partnership with a woman like us just as much as we want to connect with them. The banquet table has been set for us today. We don't need to be afraid that we won't get our fill. Now we know that denying ourselves the pleasure of sampling the types of people displayed on the table is no longer necessary. The range includes people of all ages, races, religions, professions, and physical descriptions. Today we try out what pleases us in potential partners with gusto. **I sample all potential partners with pleasure from the banquet table.**

Day 322

Kindness

I am kind to my partner. Emotional availability is kind, gentle, mild, and sympathetic. Chances are when we were stuck, and sometimes still are, we have not acted with kindness. Now exploring what kindness means to us puts us on the path to resolving our partnership issues. True kindness is benevolence and consideration. The daily practice of kindness allows us to truly love a partner. The added benefit of practicing kindness is that we feel good about our behavior. When we are kind, good-will spreads everywhere. Today we choose kindness because it allows us to have the emotionally rich partnership we crave—an emotionally available relationship. **Today I act lovingly as I interact with other people.**

Day 323

Embracing

I embrace all of my love experiences. The good, the bad, and the ugly, everything has been worthwhile. It has created this very moment. All the people in our lives have brought us gifts: knowledge of what we don't want in a relationship, spirituality, intellectual growth, treasured friends, and kind thoughts. Every relationship has taught us valuable lessons that have shaped us. When we are in pain, are grieving a relationship, or are still angry at a person from our past, it seems impossible to be grateful for something that they have given us. For example, one woman's prior partner was an avid traveler; they saw India, Nepal, and Asia together. She says that she would never have dared to travel to these exotic locations without him. She also realized from being with him how important an active and adventurous partner is to her. Even though he was not available emotionally, she received many gifts from being with him. Now looking back at the partners we have been with in the past, we clearly see the gift that each individual has given to us. Seeing the gift of all our pain and pleasure with people takes a lot of acceptance, yet holding these gifts close helps us round out our future love experiences. **I see the gift of every experience I have had with partnership.**

Day 324

Play

I love to play. When we are healing and focusing on our partnership issues with real clarity, perhaps for the first time in our lives, it can seem like all work and no play. Play and enjoyment are the most important elements of true healing, though. Without play we become dull perfectionists who just want to do this thing right, "gosh darn it." Today we know that play is essential to the well lived life. Now we use all of our creative power to bring fun into our lives. Whether playing means watching a silly movie with friends, hosting a games night, going to the comedy club, frolicking on the beach with a dog, or giving a child a hug, today we indulge in play in order to lighten our process. Now we remember why we want to partner an emotionally available person—so that we can love. **I use my creative power in order to play.**

Day 325

Completion

I am a complete person. When we are stuck in our partnership issues, we believe that we need a partner to connect us to the whole. We fear that we are separated from other people. The truth is that we are not separate; we are all interconnected. A partner can complement us; however, we do not need another person to fulfill us. Our healing process teaches us that we are complete right now. By honoring ourselves and the miracle of who we are, we know that we are complete. We don't need a partner to fulfill us. Now we uncover that complete person within us and sustain positive, healthy, loving relationships. **I celebrate my wholeness, and honor who I am.**

Day 326

Uniqueness

I maintain my uniqueness. It can be a challenge for those of us on this path, as for most women, to respect our uniqueness. Society and the media promote a cookie-cutter ideal of the feminine. But as we progress and look close up at society's images of women as if they were in a science experiment, we often discover that we don't even find the images society designates for us appealing. Freedom comes when we decide what **we** honor about being a woman. Seeking out our uniqueness and defining what our femininity looks like helps us to love ourselves. Today we search out the features we each possess that make us adorable and precious: qualities like enjoying eating with our hands, walking barefoot on a deserted beach, or delighting in a child's smile. By searching out that which makes us unique individuals, we learn that our special gifts are drawing a loving, available partnership to each of us. Emotional availability knows that we are all special and precious; now we use each day as an opportunity to honor those parts of us that make us individuals. **I explore who I am as a woman. I celebrate my uniqueness.**

Day 327

Dreams

I honor the dreams in my heart and soul. Our fears of partnership have often taken us far off course from seeing our dreams fulfilled. That is one of the real consequences of our issues. Today, though, we have the opportunity to start living our dreams. Whether our dreams involve job, lifestyle, or travel changes, this is the day to honor our heart's desire. Our relationship-related challenges stem from the idea that the right partner will make our dreams come true. Now we know better. A partner may bring us many gifts, yet we are powerful adults who honor our heart's desire. No matter what our relationship status, today we fulfill our dreams. **I take steps to make my dreams come true.**

Day 328

Winning

I am a winner. We do many wonderful things for ourselves each day. We are winners in life. Simply by getting to this place on our journey to heal our partnership issues, we are triumphing. We may associate winning with being in a partnership; however, a focus on marriage can derail us from all the miracles available to us right now. We forget that no matter what our status, simply doing this work makes us winners. We are successful every time we reconceptualize potential partners as loving beings, think of partnership, love, and sex with a sense of peace, and profoundly love ourselves. The process is what is important. We are winners today! **I enter the winner's circle as I heal my partnership issues.**

Day 329

Service

I am of service to other people. Women are taught to be great caretakers; however, there is a big difference between caretaking and being of service. Basically the difference lies in the motivation. Are we seeking love by doing for others? Are we searching for glory? Does it feel good to help someone who is in need? When we are clear about our motivation, we can be certain that we are in a service mode rather than caretaking in the hopes of getting our own needs met. Service is helping another without any expectation of reward. It feels good. The tool of service helps us as we heal our partnership issues, too, because service gets us out of ourselves. Being of help to others transfers us from being victims to being helpers. In the past, our partnership issues have made us very self-obsessed. Our self-centeredness has worked to separate us from others. Now whenever we find ourselves getting caught up in selfishness and self-centered fears, we turn our attention to what we can do to help others. **I am open to doing service for another person.**

Day 330

The Holidays

I stay present with all my feelings during the holidays. The holiday season is a time of joy and harmony, as well as an opportunity for growth. Many women get lonely at the holidays. We tend to feel left out, isolated, and hopeless, whatever our partnership status. The holidays can bring up a mix of emotions. The holiday season may be a time we consider with trepidation. Women who are single at the holidays may meet with comments about our partnership status that can be very uncomfortable. If this is the case, a planned response to parents, relatives, and friends can be useful. For women who are in partnerships, the holidays may also bring issues to the surface. Meeting our partner's family, trying to fulfill the needs of others, staying connected emotionally to the person in our lives, and being present for ourselves can present very real challenges. Whatever our situation, the holidays mark a very emotionally loaded time. Holding ourselves and knowing we will make it through the holidays is important. With gratitude for all the miracles we have in our lives, this holiday season we enjoy ourselves as we walk through our feelings. **Today I love myself through the holidays. I know that I am emotionally available.**

Day 331

Birthdays

I take especially good care of myself around my birthday. Getting older can be challenging in our society. Having a birthday can cause tremendous anxiety in women. On turning 30, 35, 40, 45, 50, 60, or 70 many of us desire to act out, desperately seek a partner, fall into depression, get fearful, or compare ourselves to where others are in life. No matter what we do, all behavior is OK. We are just fine. Although our culture prizes youth, now we know that there are many other ways of looking at aging. For example, in many cultures the elders are revered for their wisdom and life experiences. Youth is not worshipped in every culture. Today we know that we are getting better and better with each day that passes. We are becoming wiser and more loving. Now when we have a birthday coming up, we take extra-special care of ourselves. **On my birthday, I revere myself for all my wisdom and growth.**

Day 332

Power

I own my own power. Women are powerful beings. Female power can be linear, the way power is traditionally viewed in our society. Women also have powerful non-linear feminine abilities. For example, women have the power to let other people shine, the power to bring new life into the world if we choose, the power to love, and the power to nurture new life. Our power belongs to us. Although many of us may have consistently given our power to others in order to get love, we know that is no longer necessary. Now we have the chance to internalize our own power and take strength from our miraculous energy. We know that we are amazing beings with unlimited potential. Today we feel good in owning our power. **Today I rejoice in my feminine power.**

Day 333

Roots

I am firmly rooted in myself. Many of us forget that we are a part of this world. We forget that our place on the planet is special and precious. Although our challenges have gotten us into painful relationships, our issues have only manifested to teach us that we are here on this earth to have wonderful people in our lives. Today we allow our roots to grow deep into the earth. Now we create a special place for ourselves. Every day we absorb love, food, water, sunlight, nurturing, care, and attention from our essential underground source—true love. Today that love within us gives us what we need as we take root. Then we can flower in the process of loving an emotionally available partner. **I know that who I am is enough.**

Day 334

Being

I am present.

"The past is history, the future is a mystery, the present is a gift."—Eleanor Roosevelt

Being present with potential partners takes work for women healing our relationship issues. Being present means being aware and in our bodies. Our emotional shakiness functions as a running away from the moment. It manifests as a desire not to stand still and face reality. Now we know that by healing and showing up for this very moment in the present, we are creating a powerful, safe future for ourselves. The past with people is over and done with. We cannot change it. The future is a projection. Today is all we have. We have no more and no less than any other person on the planet. We are as rich in the time of this 24 hour period as the wealthiest person in the world. We have as much as anyone else. For this day only, we spend our riches wisely by being fully present with an emotionally available partner. **I celebrate myself because I am in the present moment.**

Day 335

Freedom

I am with who I want, how much, and in the way I want. Real freedom comes from choosing who we are with. Our time on this planet is precious. We deserve to spend it wisely by being with whom we want, how often we want to be with them, and in the ways that work for us. Obviously we need to respect another person's choices, too; however, we decide who we are with whenever that is possible. Being honest about who we want to be with is part of this process. Searching deeply within ourselves, and believing we deserve to be with the partner that we want, may take a lot of work for some of us to achieve. The difficulty arises because of our old ideas about other people, about partnership, and about what we deserve. We are worth the effort, though. The next step is to figure out how much time we are comfortable being with an individual. Do we want to see them only in the evenings, several times a week, or on weekends? This helps us to visualize the relationship that we want. We are important; we are worth all the work the process of healing takes. When we are on the other side of our partnership issues, we are free. **I know my imagination is powerful. I envision the relationship I want.**

Day 336

Celebration

I celebrate my healing this year.

"The only person I need to compare myself to is the person I was when I started my recovery."—Eric R.

We are on the brink of freedom. Today is a special opportunity to affirm how far we have come on our journey to heal our partnership issues. Looking back at our progress to stay present, to choose available people, and to love authentically, we claim the miracle of our healing for ourselves. Today let's list all of the positive experiences we have had on our journey so far. This day is a celebratory marker of our growth and positive movement. Right now, let's acknowledge all the work we have done and wish ourselves well. **I am ready for love.**

Chapter Summary: You are a very powerful being. You are successful right now. Congratulate yourself on a job well done. All of your work to let in an emotionally available partner is paying off. This journey is a celebration of your self-love. You are a winner!

Today make a list of 3 wonderful things you do for yourself each day. Write 2 examples of positive changes you have made since you began reading this book. Plan a time to celebrate your successes. Affirm that you are on your way to letting in the love of an emotionally available partner!

At this point, you may be enjoying a loving relationship; you may not have found your partner yet; or you may be so involved in your life that the desire to partner is less acute. No matter where you are, do not judge your process. Trust that you will experience the emotionally rich partnership that you want.

Since it is still very easy to get wrapped up in the goal of finding an emotionally available partner rather than celebrating the process, I put the next chapter on the joy of commitment last. I wanted you to get the benefit of all of the other chapters before reading this one. Successful relationships do not happen by magic. Being in a committed relationship takes a lot of work. Many women still believe in the fairy tale, but it takes daily effort to maintain a healthy partnership.

The next chapter helps you do the work necessary to sustain your relationship. It helps you to stay emotionally present for your partner when you are in a relationship. It provides essential skills for successful relating. It teaches you the joy of commitment. Now you are ready to let real love in.

·12·

The Joy of Commitment

This chapter offers you guidelines to maintaining a successful relationship. You will learn how to handle conflict, how to give your relationship a high priority on a daily basis, how to keep the focus on yourself, and how to truly share love with an emotionally available partner. Commitment is challenging, but the pay-offs are worth it. Love yourself and your partner as you indulge in the joy of commitment!

Day 337

Commitment

I am ready for a commitment. Being ready for a commitment can seem impossible. True intimacy with another person can seem too terrifying to imagine. We have many good reasons, conscious or not, restricting us from believing a committed relationship is desirable for us. We may also feel hopeless about the possibility of maintaining a relationship once we do commit to it. What we forget, though, is that the person we need to entrust ourselves to is our Self. When we care for ourselves, body, mind and soul, then we are ready for a commitment. We already know how to love naturally. We were created to share our love with others if we choose to. Doing this work just gets us ready to commit. We are well on our way! **Today I love to commit. I do it for fun!**

Day 338

Beginnings

I see every day as a new beginning to my relationship. Beginnings are wonderful. The beginning of a relationship introduces us to all of the wonder of our partner. We share, explore, and enjoy this person in front of us. Beginnings are simply one part of the process, though. Women who experience challenges in partnership often begin a relationship by getting "hooked" on the pleasure of beginnings, ignoring danger signs, giving ourselves and our power away, clinging to our partner, or shying away from intimacy. Now we know that our commitment to this healing journey means that we make a choice to let love in every day. Today we are emotionally solid as a relationship begins. Then we decide to carry on that commitment to the relationship throughout the rest of the relationship's progress. **Today I am available to begin my relationship.**

Day 339

Committing

I re-conceptualize commitment as a pleasurable experience. For many of us, commitment is terrifying. We worry about being stuck, trapped, or jilted. Commitments are fun, though, as long as we understand what we are committing to. As long as we are certain that we want to be involved with someone, we can enjoy our commitments. Commitment simply means to pledge ourselves; committing is a process of giving our love in trust to another person. Now, when we are ready to commit, we find that there are many benefits to committing. Benefits include the chance to show up, the opportunity to love a partner, and the opportunity to grow. Pledging ourselves get us out of our heads and ends our isolation. Today we re-conceptualize commitment to a person we love as a pleasurable experience. **Today I love to commit.**

Day 340

Decisions

I decide in favor of being in a relationship. For us, being in favor of a relationship with a partner takes guts. Relationships can represent fear and pain, or at least struggle, to many of us. When a person is in front of us and wants to engage in a relationship, this is the time to get closely in touch with ourselves. We can do a quick check-in by asking questions. Some sample questions are: "Do I want to relate with them? What is my motivation? Am I tempted to pull back? Is fear the motivator?" Checking in with safe friends, a therapist, or other women on this journey also assists us to decide if the relationship is important to us. Emotional availability knows that checking in with ourselves about a potential partner helps us move into an appropriate relationship when the time is right. Examining our motivation is always a wonderful tool to help us decide if we want to be in relationship with an individual. Today we go to the source—ourselves. **I am open to being in a relationship.**

Day 341

Conflict

I let go of conflict. Every couple will encounter struggles, yet many women expect the fairy tale. We rarely have well-developed skills to handle conflict. Our emotions have either sent us running from conflict in fear or have "raised our hackles." Because of our fears and issues, we have experienced relationships where we, or our partners, never let go of conflicts. If we are experiencing a challenge with our partner now, most of us do not realize that this is normal. Conflict is a part of life; everyone experiences conflict. Emotionally available partners realize that holding on to struggle is detrimental to the relationship. Healing means that we let go of conflict, act lovingly, and remember all of the reasons that we are with a person. We honor the good parts of the relationship. Today we take the lead in our relationship. For this day only, we stop indulging in conflict. **I make my relationship top priority. I let go of conflict.**

Day 342

Misunderstandings

I plan a response to misunderstandings with my partner.

"Whenever my husband or I is upset, we have this funny old pair of glasses that we put on. It is our signal that we need to remember how much we care about each other and that our misunderstanding is not as important as our relationship. Those glasses have gotten us out of some really tough situations."—Mary Jane

Misunderstandings can easily happen in a relationship due to differing expectations or communication styles. Whatever the cause, it is important to calm down and be rational when we have misunderstandings. Making a decision that the relationship takes priority, even if we are completely furious, takes a lot of discipline, though. It can help if each member of the couple agrees to use reminders beforehand. Reminders can include a silly word, an agreement to always hold hands while fighting, a decision to lie down on the bed together and just breathe, or a decision that either party can take a fifteen minute walk and **then** return. Whatever method we develop in our partnership, a jointly planned response to the inevitability of misunderstandings keeps the importance of the relationship paramount. **My partner and I make a decision that the relationship comes first today.**

Day 343

Team Members

I am on the same team as my partner. Deciding to play on a team with our partner can be challenging for us. The cultural myth is that finding the "right" partner will mean that the relationship struggle is over. Each partner will understand the other so well that the relationship will run itself. This rarely happens, though, because each player may be using a different rulebook. The concept of being team members in a relationship can help. Team members have a sense of a common goal, camaraderie, and a shared knowledge of the game's ground-rules. Each team member works together to be successful. Playing on a team is also fun. Today we know that we deserve a relationship with clear goals, common ground-rules, and two loving teammates. Now we play on the same team as our partner. **Today I take the time to gently explore with my teammate the ground-rules of our relationship. Together we win the game.**

Day 344

Day by Day

I honor my day to day, loving relationship. Today we honor the day to day process of maintaining a loving relationship, whether the relationship is with ourselves or with a partner. Healing is about putting new ideas and behaviors into practice on a daily basis. What better opportunities do we have to practice than in our significant relationships with ourselves and others? Emotional availability knows that every day is an opportunity to interact lovingly with a potential partner. This process, however, is not about perfection or martyrdom. If we find that we act in a way which is less than honorable with someone, we know that we have an opportunity each day to amend that behavior. We are not saints because we are undertaking this journey. We are simply women among women, humans among humans, who are working to honor ourselves and the person in our lives. Emotional availability knows that there is always another chance to interact lovingly with ourselves and with another person. Today we honor our partner. **I practice emotional availability today and every day.**

Day 345

Focus

I focus on my relationship. It's easy to get distracted in our world. We have thousands of channels on TV, the Internet, work, and physical fitness to distract us from our relationship. In order to have a successful partnership, though, we need to make a decision to give the relationship top priority. Successful partners usually rank their partnership number one. Many of us, however, have bought into the fairy tale idea of romance. The idea is that we will meet "that someone special" and live "happily ever after." We hope that once we find "the right person," our work is over. We think that after "The One" appears, we can move on to give attention to other areas of our lives. When this doesn't happen, we feel let down. Chasing the dream of that right relationship has been our longtime companion and scapegoat. We may have thought: "If only I could find them, then everything in my life would be OK," or "It's because I don't have a partner that my life hurts so much." Learning the truth about "happily ever after" is challenging, yet today we give our relationship the focus it deserves. Now we fan the flame of our love every day. **Today I make my relationship a top priority.**

Day 346

Sex

I ask for what I need sexually. Asking to have our sexual needs met may not be an issue for all of us; however, releasing whatever emotional baggage we have around sex can only increase our pleasure in the bedroom. Many of us still feel guilt for having sex before marriage, shame about bleeding on our menstrual cycles, and fear about sharing our needs and desires with a partner. The classification of women as either mothers or whores has lead to uncertainty in sexually intimate situations for many of us. We may also be used to pleasing our partner while deferring our own pleasure. Now we know that it helps another person please us when we clearly state what we want.

Today we get whatever support and instruction we need to communicate with our partner. (See the Bibliography for resources.) Emotional intimacy is pleasurable when we let go of our fears. Now we enjoy our sex lives. We know that we deserve to get what we need and want from sex. **Today I ask for what I need.**

Day 347

Nurturing

I nurture myself. Today we nurture ourselves. We are incredibly special and precious. We deserve good things. If we experience a lot of emotion today as we partner, we take care of ourselves appropriately. If we need to be alone, we take the space we need. If we need connection with other people, we take the steps to get our needs met. Healing is a process of getting closer to that loving, nurturing being inside of us. Loving ourselves then gives us the ability to care for our partner. The deep, sacred place inside of us knows how successful partnerships work. Our inner Self knows what we need. She is available to nurture us and the person in our lives anytime. **Today I do whatever I need to do in order to nurture myself.**

Day 348

Money

I demystify money. Money, just paper and metal, is simply a means of exchange. Real wealth is goods and services. Money is only a means to an end, yet in our culture money takes on great significance. Because money is so important, financial issues between partners can present the number one contributor to relationship challenges.

Many of us do not even like to talk about money with our partner. We fear that our financial position will turn our partner off, either because we have debt or because we make a lot of money. Money issues can seem to keep us in a catch-22. If we have money, that is an issue; if we don't have money, that is also an issue. If we have our own unresolved money issues, we may be attracted to a person who has not yet worked out their issues either. Getting to know a person's financial situation when the time is right is appropriate. We deserve a financially and emotionally available partner. We must take the steps every day to be that person, too.

Making financial decisions together is crucial for a healthy relationship. Some women feel comfortable handling our own money, others feel comfortable having our partner manage the money, and some of us favor jointly managing the finances. Money can be managed in a variety of ways. No matter what route we take in our relationship, it is OK. In the end, though, we acknowledge that money is here to serve us. Now we talk about money in healthy ways within our partnership. **I decide how I want to manage money. I clearly communicate with my partner when the time is right.**

Day 349

Giving

I give and receive unconditionally. Giving unconditionally can be very difficult for us. In the past, we often gave with the secret hope that another would love us or act appropriately because we were giving them a gift. These conditional gifts have put us in a state of "love poverty." Conditional gifts have strings attached; it is the sacrificial martyrdom of doing for others with expectations of what we **demand** in return. The answer to this quandary is to give unconditionally. To give unconditionally means letting go of our partner's response, releasing our attachment to what they choose to do with our gift, and opening ourselves to receive unconditionally. Unconditional giving is not a trade or a bargaining attempt, however. Healing our partnership issues means giving without any expectation of getting back. It means being open to receive abundance. **Today I let go of my attachments to any gift I give my partner.**

Day 350

Loving

I love slowly and gratefully. Taking our time to love someone is a rare experience. Our partnership issues are about selfishness and urgency. When we are stuck, we are not able to truly cherish those about us. We often are caught up in an external drama that is not about the relationship, such as work or family concerns. Then we are not present for our partner. Similarly, we may be stuck in old fears or engaged in future tripping. We may think thoughts such as, "I might be abandoned," or, "I won't be able to cope if my partner leaves me." Loving slowly and gratefully is the antidote to such fears.

Slow, grateful loving puts our focus back into the present moment. Going slowly with an individual allows us to revel in our partner; to love every aspect of that person, and to be grateful to have them with us. Today we explore the touch, taste, sound, smell, and sight of our partner. We thank our Higher Power for this wonderful moment of love. **Today I love to take my time with a person.**

Day 351

Progressing

I progress with a partner.

"Just do the next right thing."—Anonymous

We often run when someone wants to progress in a relationship. Whether a person is available or unavailable often makes no difference. It can be humbling for us to look back on all the missed opportunities with people who wanted to move forward with us. For example, when one woman started this process, she realized that she had shut out two available people in the last year. Then she was tempted to hate herself. Instead, she worked on her intimacy issues with the help of these principles and with a trained therapist. Now she is happy with a kind, available partner. Like her, instead of beating ourselves up, let's face the facts and realize that we want to change. Knowledge is power. Today we progress with a partner. If an appropriate person wants to move forward with us, and we feel love for them, today we do the next right thing. We walk through our fear as a mature adult with a Higher Power, the support of a therapist, or loving friends. Doing the next right thing takes courage, yet we can do it! **I love to progress with a partner.**

Day 352

Responding

I hear my partner and bounce something back to them. We were often not taught how to play fair in relationships. We are sometimes selfish; we deafen ourselves to the needs of a partner. Our needs become paramount. We may not even hear what our partner is saying. Being emotionally available means really listening to what another person says, though. Then we need to respond to them. Responding may take a tremendous amount of work for us;

just remember that as we read this book we are getting better and better. Let's trust in our process this day, practice hearing our partner, and give them a response. Today we know that availability is about being present and available to respond. We know that we are capable of "bouncing the ball back" to the person in our lives. **Today I play fair with my partner.**

Day 353

Validation

I validate my partner.

"Do unto others as you would have done unto you."—Jesus Christ

Everyone enjoys ego-strokes. For women struggling with our own fears of partnership, though, validating our partner can be hard. One woman felt so happy being with her partner that she thought her heart would burst. Even though she felt so full of love, she was afraid to tell the truth. One day, she took a big breath and told her love how she felt. Her partner was thrilled! Like this woman, we can be honest with our partners. Letting go of all our fears, taking the time, and mustering the energy to validate our partners may take some practice; yet it is possible. Spending some quiet time reflecting on the well-grounded reasons for our being with someone helps us. Once we are clear about our connection to another person, we more easily express our love for them. With daily practice as we heal, we are getting better and better at validating the person in our lives. **For this day only, I share what I find meaningful and relevant about a potential partner.**

Day 354

Rights

I have the right to my own time and my own life. Resolving our partnership issues means that we reclaim our own lives and time. Today we use our limited time wisely. When a potential partner wants more time than we feel comfortable giving them, we look closely at ourselves and at the partnership. If we find that a person's needs are valid, then we amend our behavior and let go of some external commitments that may be consuming us. We come into balance by being more physically and emotionally available. If we feel that they are asking for us to give up more than we are comfortable with or are able to let go of, that is another thing. We may feel we cannot or do not want to give more of ourselves to the relationship. At that point, negotiation and boundary setting can be helpful tools. Whatever course we take in our partnerships, today we hold our own time, and time with our partner, in balance. **Today I know that my relationship has room for my own time and my own life.**

Blessing My Partner

I bless this person. Women have very intense, complicated relationships with people. We are constantly fed a great array of information that castigates others. People are not villains, though; in fact, human beings are to be venerated. Our partners deserve to be loved for more than the traditional qualities we were taught to admire. Today we love others not because they are great providers; now we clearly see that they are blessed simply because they inhabit this beautiful earth with us. What a concept! When we are with our partner, we actually revere them as a precious creation in the world just like us. They are a gift from the universe. Loving them is a blessed occasion. Now we know that by re-conceptualizing what love means to us, we heal ourselves, our partners, and our world. **Today I see love experiences with my partner as a wonderful way to truly honor life.**

Responsibility

Responsibility equals the ability to respond. Being an equal partner feels good, yet we may fear responsibility. In our past relationships, many of us were incapable of responding to our partners. Now when a person asks a question or raises an issue, we reply; we give feedback in answer. We match a partner each step of the way in a relationship. However, the responsibility of being an adult and "bouncing the ball back" to another person can be very uncomfortable for some of us. It may still seem easier to just not respond. If we put two and two together, though, we see that responsibility equals the ability to give feedback to our partner. The more practice we get at taking responsibility for our role in the relationship, the more closeness and love we participate in. Today we are capable of responding appropriately to a partner.

We re-conceptualize responsibility as a joy that we lovingly attend to in our partnership each day. **Today I respond to a potential partner for fun.**

Day 357

My Opinion

I voice my opinion in front of others about things outside of myself.

"My therapist told me to read the newspaper every day and to let my partner know how I feel about current events."—Tami

Our partnership issues work in extremes—we either scorch someone with our opinion, or we are unwilling to let them know what we think. Being available means that we let other people see us; however, many of us get so overwhelmed by outside events that we shut down to anything that doesn't directly concern us. We also may fear that no one will be interested in our opinion. Today we acknowledge that shutting down and wondering why we should bother to tell our partner how we experience life is evidence of our partnership issues. We know that letting someone see us is gift that we give to them. Being visible is a choice to be emotionally available. With great courage, today we reveal ourselves. **I tell my partner how I experience external events.**

Day 358

All Is Well

I have a loving, harmonious relationship with my partner. All is well. Our society revels in drama. We often hear about relationships that are going through changes, strife, and problems. We don't usually hear about partnerships that are progressing smoothly. Now, whenever we are obsessing on our relationship when that is not called for, when we are bored, or when dramas play out in our heads when things are actually fine, we know that something else is going on. By delving into our feelings, we discover the real source of our anxiety. Then we choose to see the harmony in our relationships. Today we entertain ourselves without drama. We check in with safe friends or seek professional help to let go of anxiety. Making a choice to be in harmony can be very uncomfortable for us, but we can do it. **I abstain from all obsessive thoughts and dramas about my relationship that play**

200 / The Emotionally Available Partner

out in my head today.

Future Plans

I include my partner in my future plans. When we are stuck in our fears, we leave another person out of our future plans. We do this because we believe no one will ever stick around. We think that we must protect ourselves from abandonment. We may also exclude them because they are too needy, available, or eager; we don't want to be "smothered!"

Now we know that healing our partnership issues is about balance. Healing calls for letting appropriate people in when the time is opportune and making a decision to stay together if the fit is right. Healing is characterized by giving an available person an indication that we will hang in there awhile. We do not have to commit for eternity, yet we do need to let a significant person know that we see a place for them in our future plans. **For this day only, I link my future with that of my partner.**

Moving Forward

I take a forward course of action with a partner.

"Just do the next right thing."—Anonymous

Many of us have resisted taking the next step with a partner. When our partner wanted to move forward, many of us have sabotaged the relationship. We have hung back, or actually fled the partnership. The reasons we have declined to move forward were sometimes because we knew we shouldn't be in the relationship. Most often, though, we held back because we feared we would lose ourselves if we committed to our partner. Whatever we choose to do with our partner is OK, progressing or holding back; however, today we know that moving forward with them is necessary if we love them. If we need support to move to the next level with our partner, now we get help. (See the Bibliography for ideas.) Healing is about walking through our fears and taking the next right action. Today we know that progress feels good. It moves us closer to our partner, not further away from ourselves. **I love to progress** with my partner today.

Asking for What I Want

I state the quality of relationships I want. The common theory in our culture is that a woman who asks for what she wants threatens people. Real relationships take honesty, though. A woman who doesn't state her truth often ends up in unfulfilling relationships. That is the ultimate threat to our well-being. Our partners also suffer when we are unclear about what we need. Now knowing that our happiness radiates out to everyone helps us decide in favor of joy. Instead of making another person play guessing games, today we state what we need in a relationship. Not everyone will meet us when we ask for what we want, yet we can trust that there are people who want to hear our truth. Now we have the ability to understand timing as well; therefore, in an opportune moment we ask for what we want in a relationship. **Today I release all fear about how others will react. I state the quality of relationships I want.**

Emotional Responsibility

I accept the emotional responsibility of a relationship.

"Adulthood is overrated."—Marina

It isn't always pleasurable to have to be an adult. We face many demands. Relationships take lots of investment. Being intimate with a partner takes work; it is a large commitment. Because we sometimes shy away from doing work, showing up, and being accountable, we forget that intimacy is worth the effort. By gaining some clarity about what our partnership issues are doing to us, though, we see that our immaturity hurts us. It keeps us from the relationship we want; we wouldn't be reading this book if it didn't. The choice to be in relationship with an emotionally available partner means that every day we are answerable for our part. With courage and trust, today we accept the challenge of being accountable for all our feelings. Now we gratefully do the work of being an adult. **For the next 24 hours, I am open to being responsible in a relationship.**

Expectations

I live up to the realistic expectations of my partner. When we are stuck, we either expect far too much from ourselves in relationships or we try to get away with substandard treatment of another person. Usually we have no idea what is practical in partnerships. For example we may expect 100% from our partner 24/7. This is not realistic. Giving 80% is the realistic percentage we learn now. No human can give 100% in a relationship. Whether we talk to a counselor, a trusted friend, or a spiritual advisor, we determine what is realistic in our relationship. We do not abuse or criticize ourselves for the ways that we have been acting; however, we live up to our partner's expectations if they make sense. **I get clear and balanced to determine realistic expectations for a relationship.**

Day 364

You Can Count on Me

My partner can count on me.

"Suit up and show up."—Anonymous

Our partnership issues take the form of not being able to show up for tough situations. We may have truly wanted to be there for our partner; however, our own selfishness, self-consciousness, and/or anger have blocked our ability to be counted on in the past. Today we know that learning to be present is essential. The process of healing our relationship issues means that we suit up and show up for our partner. Then, as we practice showing up, we experience how good it feels to release from our own issues for the good of the partnership. We learn that the power of giving to another person provides us with great pleasure. **For today, I am a person to be counted on.**

Day 365

Marriage

I know that marriage is a decision made by two people to live as partners. Marriage is a social institution that formalizes the decision of two people to live together. In our society, marriage takes on tremendous significance because it is a legal or religious ceremony that signifies connection. Marriage is a cultural obsession. People feel very strongly about marriage. Marriage is either outdated and a pain, or it is essential for a well-lived life. We may have many ideas about marriage; we may fear it or crave it. Marriage in itself, however, is basically just a formal decision of two people to live together. Today we give marriage less power. We know that marriage in itself is simply a symbol of the decision made by two equal partners. **I demystify marriage by realizing that it is a merger of two adult people.**

Chapter Summary: Now you have a better understanding of the work that goes into a committed relationship. Just because you have made it this far doesn't mean that you are a heroine, a princess, or a saint, though. This is the journey of everywoman. You are a woman among women. At this point you accept that things are not always blissful in your emotionally available partnership. You see that ups and downs are normal.

If you are in a relationship, be kind to yourself. If you make a "mistake" and are tempted to judge yourself at any time, think about where you were when you started this process. Look at all of your progress toward commitment. Remember that there is always another chance to love your partner well.

If you haven't found your life-mate at this time, don't despair. Ask yourself questions instead of wondering when it will happen for you. Ask: "What can I do to let go of my obsession with finding a life-mate? What can I do to start to live my life right now? What are some ways I can take care of myself physically, emotionally, and spiritually?"

Now you know that when you let go of the constant worry of finding and keeping a mate, then you make room for the energy needed to take care of yourself. Being with an emotionally present person takes a lot of work. It **is** scary; however, the pay-offs are great. No matter where you are in your process of letting love in, by making it to this point you have accomplished a great deal. Your work is worthwhile. You are now on the other side!

Phase IV Summary: Congratulate yourself on a truly amazing year! You have come far on your journey to release your partnership issues. During this phase you have learned how to love the spiritual part of yourself, how to celebrate your successes on this journey, and how to commit powerfully to a relationship. You are now enjoying true power and freedom.

At this point you find that you have more faith in yourself. You know that even if your partnership does not work out, you will be taken care of. You experience your personal worth, no matter what your partnership status. You esteem yourself—with or without a partner. You love every part of yourself, and you love others.

As you finish **Phase IV** and conclude this book, give yourself the recognition you deserve. You are a powerful, free woman. Remember that your example speaks to the millions of women still struggling with their partnership issues. Your freedom frees others. Share what you have learned. Embrace yourself. Most importantly, have fun! An emotionally rich partnership is your birthright. In this moment, applaud all your progress to letting in the love of an emotionally available partner. You are ready for love!

Conclusion

A few years ago a book titled *The Rules* came out. *The Rules* supplies women with complete instructions for finding and nabbing a partner. It is appealing because it offers a "formula" for women searching for "The One." National women's magazines, newspapers, advertisements, and many other books piggyback on the relationship "formula" presented in *The Rules*. All of these powerful influences provide women with relationships tricks and trademarks that make "the prize" seem easy to attain, and what woman doesn't want that? The only catch is that women need to pretend to be someone we are not. But what's so challenging about that when we women have already been taught to hide our true selves from the world forever?

The Emotionally Available Partner: A Journey to True Love offers an antidote to hiding ourselves. As we journeyed through this book, we learned in stages about ourselves, about other people, about emotional maturity, and about the power and freedom of overlooking the seductive relationship "formula." As a result, we have discovered that we are already the emotionally available partner that we seek; that we integrally know how to love naturally; and that we let love in every time we are true to our Self. At this point, we know that women do not need to pretend to be someone else in order to love a great partner well. We also know that if we do pretend, sooner or later our masks slip. Most importantly, we know that we already have an internal guide who doesn't need pretense.

Relationships matter. Our journey has led us to understand that the denial of our true selves in relationships is not effective, appropriate, or pleasurable. We have discovered that each time we deny our true selves, ignore our intuition, make partnership more important than self-care, and falsely represent ourselves to potential partners, we are vanishing. We don't want to vanish anymore. We want to enjoy our power—the power of being a woman who knows herself completely. Even though it has been a hard journey, our challenges in intimate relationships have brought us closer to ourselves. Through healing our partnership issues, we have accessed our power.

Now we make powerful choices about what we want. Not every woman craves a relationship. Not every woman wants to be in partnership with an emotionally available person; however, *The Emotionally Available Partner: A*

Journey to True Love tells those of us who do that we already have within all that is needed to sustain a healthy relationship. We understand that we do not need to hide our magnificence any longer. We do not need to deny our truth. We also do not need to give up and pretend that we really don't want to partner. We have a choice—the choice to do what works for **us**.

After our year of diligent work, we know a lot more about how to let in an emotionally available partner. We have learned how to recognize red flags, how to listen to our intuition, and how to honor wherever we are in our process. Now we choose partners who meet our needs. We listen to our own "rules." We are free. We are the emotionally available partner.

Bibliography

Bradshaw, John. *Healing the Shame that Binds You.* Deerfield, FL: Health Communications, 1988.

Bryant, Roberta Jean. *Stop Improving Yourself and Start Living.* San Rafael, CA: New World Library, 1991.

Callan, Dawn. *Awakening the Warrior Within: Secrets of Personal Safety and Inner Security.* Novato, CA: Nataraj Publishing, 1995.

Collins, Bryn C. *Emotional Unavailability: Recognizing It, Understanding It, and Avoiding Its Trap.* Chicago, IL. Contemporary Books, 1997.

Conway, Diane. *The Fairy Godmother's Guide to Dating and Mating.* San Rafael, CA: BookPartners, Inc., 1997.

Ellis, Albert and Ted Crawford. *Making Intimate Connections: Seven Guidelines for Great Relationships and Better Communication.* Atascadero, CA: Impact Publishers, 2000.

Estes, Clarissa Pinkola. *Women Who Run with the Wolves: Myths and Stories of the Wild Woman Archetype.* New York: Ballantine, 1992.

Gilman, Susan Jane. *Kiss My Tiara: How to Rule the World as a SmartMouth Goddess.* New York: Warner Books, 2001.

Herman, Judith Lewis. *Trauma and Recovery: The Aftermath of Violence—From Domestic Abuse to Political Terror.* New York: BasicBooks, 1992.

Johnson, Karen. *Trusting Ourselves: The Complete Guide to Emotional Well-Being for Women.* New York: Atlantic Press, 1990.

Leonard, Linda Schierse. The *Wounded Woman: Healing the Father-Daughter Relationship.* Boston, MA: Shambhala, 1985.

Lerner, Harriet Goldhor. *The Dance of Anger: A Woman's Guide to Changing the Pattern of Intimate Relationships.* New York: Bantam Books, 1993.

_____. The *Dance of Intimacy: A Woman's Guide to Courageous Acts of Change in Key Relationships*. New York: Harper & Row, 1986.

McKay, Matthew and Patrick Fanning. *Self-Esteem*. New York: St. Martin's Press, 1988.

McKay, Matthew, Martha Davis and Patrick Fanning. *Messages: The Communication Skills Book*. Oakland, CA: New Harbinger Publications, 1983.

Miller, Alice. *The Drama of the Gifted Child: The Search for the True Self*. New York: Basic Books, 1994.

Muir, Charles and Caroline Muir. *Tantra: The Art of Conscious Loving*. San Francisco: Mercury House, 1990.

Normandi, Carol Emery and Lauralee Roark. *It's Not About Food: End Your Obsession with Food and Weight*. New York: Perigee, 1998.

Prather, Hugh. *Notes to Myself: My Struggle to Become a Person*. New York: Bantam Books, 1976.

Roth, Geneen. *When Food Is Love: Exploring the Relationship Between Eating and Intimacy*. New York: Penguin Books, 1991.

Sark. *The Bodacious Book of Succulence: Daring to Live Your Succulent Wild Life!* New York: Fireside, 1998.

Steinem, Gloria. *The Revolution from Within: A Book of Self-Esteem*. Boston: Little, Brown & Co., 1992.

Index

ABOUT THE AUTHOR

Marian Lindner is an author and relationship coach who lives and works in Northern California. Her research on emotional availability has helped a great many men and women achieve fulfillment in relationships. She lives in Marin County with her very emotionally available husband, Charles, and their daughter, Sophie.

Made in the USA
Charleston, SC
20 December 2015